D1553208

Ethical Norms,
Particular Cases

Ethical Norms, Particular Cases

JAMES D. WALLACE

Cornell University Press

ITHACA AND LONDON

Copyright © 1996 by Cornell University

First published 1996 by Cornell University Press.

Library of Congress Cataloging-in-Publication Data
Wallace, James D., 1937–
    Ethical norms, particular cases
    James D. Wallace.
        p. cm.
    Includes bibliographical references and index.
    ISBN 0–8014–3213–8 (cloth : alk. paper)
    1. Ethics. 2. Practice (Philosophy) 3. Authority. I. Title.
    BJ1031.W29 1996
    171'.2—dc20   96–5043

Printed in the United States of America

⊗ The paper in this book meets the minimum requirements
of the American National Standard for Information Sciences—
Permanence of Paper for Printed Library Materials, ANSI Z39.48–1984.

To My Mother and Father
Jane P. Wallace
Donald F. Wallace

Contents

Preface

Practical knowledge is obviously the result of people's cumulative experience in coping with the particular problems they encounter. We learn from others how to do things, we seek and cultivate better and more effective ways of doing them, and we transmit this knowledge to others. Know-how and practical norms—standards of better and worse ways of doing things—are in this sense human creations based upon our experience. The norms that originate in this way derive their authority from the activities they constitute and from their role in facilitating the purposes the activities serve. The aim of this book is to present an account of ethics that emphasizes the similarities between moral and other kinds of practical knowledge. Morality is presented as a collection of disparate items of practical knowledge that have their origin and authority in the learned activities that are the substance of our lives. The result is a naturalistic account of ethics that understands moral knowledge as straightforwardly empirical.

Morality, so conceived, will reflect a quite particular history. It will have been formed by the particular problems people have encountered and the actual successes and failures experienced in dealing with them. The understanding of a moral consideration will require an understanding of the particular sort of problems that occasioned its development. This view suggests that morality, like any kind of practical knowledge, is changeable, improvable. A changing world presents us with unprecedented ethical problems, and morality is our resource for devising and crafting solutions. In the process, morality is changed and sometimes improved.

Preface

Such a view of ethics promises a relatively unproblematic account of the origin and the source of authority of moral norms. It indicates a way of understanding how properly to resolve difficult moral problems. It will seem at the outset to many readers, however, to involve an unacceptable conventionalism and relativism. I promise these readers that in what follows I have not neglected their concerns.

The present book began in an effort to respond to formal commentaries on an earlier work of mine generously provided by my colleagues William Schroeder and David Shwayder. It subsequently grew in several directions, continuing, as it had started, as responses to the promptings of others. Philosophical audiences at various meetings of the American Philosophical Association and at Cornell University made useful comments on earlier versions of parts of the work. Marcia Baron, Robert McKim, Dennis Patterson, Amelie Rorty, Allen Wood, and a reader for the Cornell University Press provided helpful written comments at various stages.

The Program for the Study of Cultural Values and Ethics at the University of Illinois at Urbana-Champaign provided support in 1991–92 in the form of a fellowship. The program sponsored an interdisciplinary faculty seminar on Ethics in Careers and Professions that met regularly for two years. I benefited greatly from the opportunity to discuss many issues and examples with the seminar. Walter Feinberg was particularly helpful and encouraging in this undertaking.

Much of the material in this work was presented and discussed in two graduate seminars at UIUC in Spring 1992, and Fall 1993. I thank the participants in those discussions.

My chief intellectual debt is to Frederick L. Will. This study is an attempt to apply to some issues in ethics his conception of norms of thought and action as set out in several places, including his book *Beyond Deduction*. I am deeply grateful for the stimulus of his work and for his encouragement.

Blackwell Publishers have given permission to reprint in Chapter 2 material that originally appeared under the title "Theorizing about Morals," *Nous* 25 (1991), 176–83. Chapter 5 is a revised version of "Morality, Practical Knowledge, and Will," which appeared in *Jour-*

nal of Philosophical Research 19 (1994), 23–36, and is used with the permission of the Philosophy Documentation Center, publisher of *Journal of Philosophical Research*.

For her loving support and for her invaluable editorial assistance, I thank my wife, Sally Foster Wallace.

JAMES D. WALLACE

Urbana, Illinois

1. Introduction: Particularism and Pluralism

> The concrete situation is almost everything.
>
> Heraclitus was right, things cannot stand still.

These two quotations from Isaiah Berlin's magisterial essay "The Pursuit of the Ideal" can serve as mottoes for the pluralist, particularist view of ethics I defend in the pages that follow. In this essay, published in 1988, and in "The Decline of Utopian Ideas in the West," published ten years earlier, Berlin's emphasis is historical and political. He considers the twentieth century, which his life nearly spans, and asks what historians in the future will find distinctive about the period.[1] He notes the scientific and technological successes, but Berlin is particularly struck by the violent "ideological storms" that occasioned unprecedented suffering and destruction in this century. He argues that ideas played important roles in these events and concludes that we should content ourselves with relatively modest aims in politics.

His position is based in part on a certain philosophical conception of value and a view about the nature of practical problems generally. In the course of arguing for his historical thesis, Berlin indicates a view about how people properly deal with practical problems. An important element in this view is what Berlin calls "pluralism," the

---

1. These two essays are published in Isaiah Berlin, *The Crooked Timber of Humanity*, ed. Henry Hardy (New York: Vintage Books, 1990), pp. 1–19 and 20–48. Unless otherwise indicated, numbers in the text in parentheses refer to pages in this book.

theses that [1] human beings pursue many different goods, *and* [2] these many goods are not simultaneously realizable. Berlin says he first learned about pluralism from Machiavelli, who suggested that the aims of rulers whose goals are those of the Roman Republic are different from and incompatible with the aims of Christianity (8). Incompatible, too, are the forms of life that people lead in trying to achieve such different aims and some of the personal qualities needed to succeed in these various enterprises. The various goods human beings pursue are not simultaneously realizable because they are different and incompatible (31).

One of the central assumptions of much Western political thought, Berlin says, is that there exist true immutable, universal, timeless, objective values valid for all people everywhere at all times: values that are, at least in principle, simultaneously realizable in a coherent system that would, conceived in social terms, constitute the perfect society (5–6, 25). Berlin calls this "a Platonic ideal"; I will refer to it as Plato's thesis.

Pluralism, which includes the claim that all goods are not simultaneously realizable, is important because it contradicts Plato's thesis, a thesis that continues to be very influential. In its most general form, as Berlin formulates it, Plato's thesis claims that there is some single harmonious composite of all goods, one that we can conceive and pursue even though we may be unable to attain it. This thesis underlies various utopias that have been described. It belongs with a cluster of assumptions: [1] to all genuine questions, there is but one true answer, all other answers being false; [2] a method exists for the discovery of these correct answers; and [3] all the correct answers to the many questions are compatible with one another and perhaps systematically interconnected (23–24). So these assumptions imply that all the correct answers to questions about how people should live and how communities should be organized are compatible with one another and perhaps systematically interconnected.

> Truths [about how people should live] will logically entail one another in a single, systematic, interconnected whole; at the very least, they will be consistent with one another: that is, they will form a harmonious whole, so that when you have discovered all the correct answers to all the central questions of human life and

put them together, the result will form a kind of scheme of the sum of knowledge needed to lead a—or rather the—perfect life. (25)

Berlin claims that human experience, revealed in comparisons of various cultures in various historical periods, supports pluralism and not the Platonic thesis. The writings of the eighteenth-century Neapolitan professor of rhetoric Giambattista Vico and the eighteenth-century German critic of the Enlightenment Johann Gottfried Herder present such comparisons of cultures. The experience of individuals, too, might be cited in support of Berlin's claim. We expect to forgo certain undeniable goods in order to pursue others; such, it appears, is the human condition.

> The world in which what we see as incompatible values are not in conflict is a world altogether beyond our ken; . . . principles which are harmonized in this other world are not the principles with which, in our daily lives, we are acquainted; if they are transformed, it is into conceptions not known to us on earth. But it is on earth that we live, and it is here that we must believe and act. (13)

What, then, accounts for the attractiveness of the Platonic thesis? There is, of course, the power and beauty of the philosophy of Plato, but there is more to it than that. What inclines us to the Platonic thesis, it seems to me, is the belief that what Berlin calls pluralism—the view that the many goods are not simultaneously realizable—undermines the effectiveness of intelligence and reasonableness as guides in practical affairs. The fear is that irrationalism follows if we reject the Platonic view of the systematic harmony of all goods.

There are indications that Aristotle saw that the Platonic thesis does not accord well with prominent facts about human life, but at the same time, he sought to describe *the* good for man. The *Nicomachean Ethics* can be read, I think, as Aristotle's unsuccessful attempt to reconcile the Platonic thesis with these prominent facts.

How can there be reasonableness in practical matters if goods are irreducibly many and not all harmonizable with one another? In this case, would not one have simply to choose some good without any reason and pursue it? What, other than subjective considerations, naked preferences, could indicate that one should opt for one good rather than another or stick with any one after choosing it? Apparently, if pluralism is true, one's plight is that of Plato's "democratic" individual.

> He lives on, yielding day by day to the desire at hand. Sometimes he drinks heavily while listening to the flute; at other times, he drinks only water and is on a diet; sometimes he goes in for physical training; at other times, he's idle and neglects everything; and sometimes he even occupies himself with what he takes to be philosophy. He often engages in politics, leaping up from his seat and saying and doing whatever comes into his mind. If he happens to admire soldiers, he's carried in that direction, if money-makers, in that one. There's neither order nor necessity in his life.[2]

Berlin has no intention of endorsing such erratic caprice. His solution to the problem of how, if pluralism holds, intelligence can effectively direct choice can be understood as implying a general view of reasonableness in practical matters—an account of practical reasoning. The view is described obliquely through an exposition of the ideas of Vico and Herder.

Berlin finds the following in Vico and Herder (8–10): Different cultures have different aims. A people such as the Homeric Greeks pursue a particular set of goods and struggle to harmonize these. This fact about a culture characterizes it, colors its activities and institutions in ways that make its way of life quite special and particular; the fact makes it different from all other cultures. Yet the distinctive set of goods that each culture cultivates are, for all that, recognizable as human goods. The aims and way of life of each culture can be understood by those from other cultures. Yet the possibility of one culture's pursuing certain goods that are aimed at by another culture may be foreclosed because of the incompatibility of these latter goods with other goods embedded in the first culture. So, one could not live the life of a Bronze Age Achaean and at the same time pursue Aristotle's contemplative life or the Christian Kingdom of Heaven.

---

2. *Republic* 561 C-D. The translation is from Plato, *Republic*, trans. G. M. A. Grube, revised by C. D. C. Reeve (Indianapolis, Ind.: Hackett, 1992), p. 232.

Not only do ways of life characteristic of whole cultures involve the pursuit of certain goods and the necessary forgoing of other genuine goods. Individuals within cultures are faced by the same fact of the incompatibility of the many goods they, as individuals, might reasonably cultivate. Berlin says that he has no idea of how to answer questions asked in the abstract about what goods should be pursued and which forgone, about which goods are more important. He notes, however, that "in concrete contexts, not every claim is of equal force" (17).

One important point is that which goods can be combined or harmonized and which of them is most important often depends upon what the concrete situation, the local context (including its social aspect) will allow. So, in happy circumstances, one can discharge one's obligations as a citizen of a particular community, one can pursue *a* career (though probably not several), one can cultivate amiable relations with other people, and one can participate lovingly in a domestic life. In Sartre's famous example, the Nazi occupation of France had made it impossible for a certain young man to combine these things.[3] He was forced to choose among them, to decide whether to escape to England to join the resistance movement and oppose the oppressors or to stay at home with his mother, whose other son had been killed and who was completely dependent upon him. Stuart Hampshire resists the view that this young person must simply choose without any grounds for choice.

> These are two different ways of life, because they demand different dispositions and habits of mind, different social settings, and different ends of action. . . . The choice between the two ways of life, with their constitutive virtues and defects, is open to reflection and to discussion: which virtues are incompatible with each other, under present and foreseeable social conditions and in the light of what is known of psychology and of ordinary human experience, past and present? Are the repugnant features, different in each way of life, ineliminable? Is a commitment to one of the two irreversible? Are both ways of life likely to endure indefinitely, or does one of them, at least, depend on social and political conditions that

---

3. Jean-Paul Sartre, *Existentialism and Humanism*, trans. P. Mairet (Brooklyn, N.Y.: Haskell House, 1977), pp. 35–37.

> are temporary? These are just a few of the questions that are likely to be relevant. There would not be an undiscussible issue . . . leaving the subject blankly staring at stark alternatives with nothing more to be said.[4]

People faced with such a choice should consider, in addition to the matters Hampshire mentions, whether their particular personal qualities will enable them to live one of these lives more successfully than the other—some people would be unable successfully to play the role of a docile subject of tyrants, while others would be incapable of the violence and deceit necessary to be an effective resistance fighter. It would be relevant to consider whether and how far one's contribution to either cause would be likely to be appreciable. An actual problem of this kind may offer an abundance of practical considerations that are relevant to an intelligent choice, but these considerations lie in the particular circumstances, the facts about the situation, including its antecedents and its probable results. An investigation of certain particulars is what is called for here.

In response to the question, how can one choose between incompatible goods in a way that is reasonable rather than arbitrary, Berlin responds that he knows of no way of doing this in the abstract. We should consider, though, some particular concrete situation where such a problem arises. There we will find some more or less difficult practical problem, but with some ground to stand on and with some idea of how one might reasonably seek to resolve such a problem. It is with this point in mind that Berlin says, "The concrete situation is almost everything" (18).

This notion, that the concrete context in which a practical problem arises is an indispensable determinant of an intelligent solution, makes Heraclitus's point important. The world continually presents us with new, unprecedented circumstances. If the situation itself is an important determinant of reasonable choice and action, and if we continually face novel circumstances, then it is unlikely that our past successes in solving problems will yield a method that will automatically suffice for the resolution of future problems. Yet it seems that our resources for solving unprecedented problems must lie

4. Stuart Hampshire, *Two Theories of Morality* (Oxford: Oxford University Press, 1971), pp. 37–39.

somehow in our past experience with other problems. Berlin does not address this issue, but it is an important one for the sort of view he adopts. The issue will occupy a central place in the chapters that follow.

If we accept pluralism, Berlin concludes, we are not committed to groundless choices, but we must also content ourselves with relatively modest political goals.

> It is not a matter of purely subjective judgment: it is dictated by the forms of life of the society to which one belongs, a society among other societies, with values held in common, whether or not they are in conflict, by the majority of mankind throughout recorded history. There are, if not universal values, at any rate a minimum without which societies could scarcely survive. . . . But on the other hand, the search for perfection does seem to me a recipe for bloodshed, no better even if it is demanded by the sincerest of idealists, the purest of heart. (18)

Berlin declines to call this version of pluralism "relativism," on the grounds that the aims pursued by different cultures remain recognizable as human goods and the ways of life are all intelligible to each of us (10–11). *One* of the reasons for the ideological storms of this century is connected with the widespread belief that one cannot expect understanding or accommodation with peoples whose cultures are different. If adherents of such a view at the same time hold that their own way of life can be transmuted by some plan of action into a utopia that is the realization of the Platonic ideal of a harmonious composite of all goods, then it is tempting for them to suppose that they must effect their plan by any and all means necessary. The destruction and suffering occasioned by the execution of the plan is justified by the projected end; the horrors are the eggs broken in making the sublime omelet (15–16).

The views that values are irreducibly plural and sometimes incompatible (pluralism) and that attention to the concrete circumstances in which practical problems arise is necessary for the intelligent solution of such problems (particularism) indicate a certain understanding of practical knowledge. On the latter view, such knowledge consists in an accumulation of ways of solving problems that experience has shown to be better rather than worse for certain purposes. Since the experiences that produced this knowledge were particular and concrete, it would not be surprising to discover that the knowledge itself is closely tied to particular historical situations. Because we are social beings who educate one another, we would expect such knowledge to be connected with particular social situations, and at the same time to be cultivated and shared. Such practical knowledge includes matters classified as moral.

How such practical knowledge, which must somehow embrace purposes and norms, can be empirical in this way requires explanation. The place of ethics in this conception needs to be explained, as does the mechanism for the criticism, correction, and revision of practical and moral knowledge so conceived. In the account that follows, practical considerations, including ethical values and norms, are treated as components of one or more socially established practices guided by a body of empirical practical knowledge. The practices and the associated knowledge are understood as historical phenomena—as a group of people's cumulative knowledge of how to deal with certain kinds of problems they have encountered. A Heraclitan world presents them with novel concrete problems, and their practical knowledge, based upon experience with a limited number of other, different concrete situations, must somehow suffice.

2. Morality and Practical Knowledge

1

I take seriously the ancient idea that what we call morality is a body of practical knowledge, analogous in important ways to such things as navigation, law, agriculture, medicine, chess, and music. One may entertain this hypothesis without forgetting that there are important differences between being a person of good character and being a good navigator, farmer, physician, and so on. For the moment, I wish to emphasize the similarities among all of these things. In the present philosophical context, influenced as it is by Aristotle and Kant, there is little danger that it will be forgotten that there are differences.

Bodies of practical knowledge are human creations, artifacts, the cumulative result of the repeated application of people's intelligence to practical problems that arise in their activities. These social and intellectual artifacts are meant to serve people's needs and interests, though, as with any human creation, they may not be as effective and efficient as people would like. The character at any particular time of a body of practical knowledge such as medicine or music is the result of historical circumstances. One can master a body of practical knowledge without learning its history, but the explanation of why music is as it is at the moment is to be found in the history of music.

The development of a body of practical knowledge can be a very complex matter. Understanding such a history will involve understanding the development of a certain area of human interest. As people have learned how to do certain things, their conception of what can be done has enlarged. Their goals have developed accordingly, often in the direction of greater and greater complexity. At the same time, the standards by which activities are judged as done well or poorly change, too. We will be able to discern in such a history certain clear successes and failures. It may also appear to us that there are periods in which the activity that is the subject of the history flourishes and others in which it is in decline. Such judgments, however, can be difficult and controversial. Is serial music an advance or an aberration? Perhaps it is too early to tell. There are, however, special difficulties in assessing the activities of more remote times. Historians of science know that it is a mistake to evaluate past practice of scientific inquiry and its results simply in terms of its similarity to our own current practice and its results. At other times, the world was different, and people's interests and problems were unlike our own. The divergence of their practice from our own may have been dictated by differences in their problems and purposes. Judgments about how successful they were in their practice, in any area, should take account of their problems and interests as they understood them, but taking account of such matters will require considerable effort and imagination.[1]

If we study the development of a certain area of practical knowledge, it is sometimes apparent that as technique for the activity improves, the notion of the point or purpose of the activity becomes more complex and refined. The purpose of the activity thus changes, but often in ways that seem a natural development of potentialities present in earlier forms of the activity. Paralleling such a development will be a development of the standards by which performances of the activity are judged to be better or worse. Alasdair MacIntyre illustrates such a development with a sketch of the history of portrait painting in Europe from the Middle Ages through the seventeenth century. Originally, a certain person—St. Peter or Christ—was given some human face with an expression of an appropriate emotion or attribute, but the question of whether the painted face resembled the face of the particular person did not arise. By the fifteenth century, painters began to strive for natural-

---

1. See, for example, Thomas S. Kuhn, *The Structure of Scientific Revolutions* (Chicago: University of Chicago Press, 1962), chap. 1.

ism, and the point was to create a likeness of a particular human face. Rembrandt later achieved a synthesis of naturalistic portrait and icon by revealing character in a likeness of a particular face. Successive portrait painters tended to "extend" (MacIntyre's apt word) the aims of portrait painting; technique and purpose evolved together.[2] As the conception of the purpose of portrait painting develops, the understanding of what it is to succeed at the activity, to do well at the activity, changes and develops. The norms of excellence of the activity develop too.

In his 1922 book *Human Nature and Conduct*, John Dewey made the same general point about language.

> Language grew out of unintelligent babblings, instinctive motions called gestures, and the pressure of circumstance. But nevertheless language once called into existence is language and operates as language. It operates not to perpetuate the forces which produced it but to modify and redirect them. It has such transcendent importance that pains are taken with its use. Literatures are produced, and then a vast apparatus of grammar, rhetoric, dictionaries, literary criticism, reviews, essays, a derived literature *ad lib*. Education, schooling, becomes a necessity; literacy an end. In short, language when it is produced meets old needs and opens new possibilities. It creates demands which take effect, and the effect is not confined to speech and literature, but extends to the common life in communication, counsel and instruction.

Dewey generalized this point.

> Each institution has brought with its development demands, expectations, rules, standards. These are not mere embellishments of the forces which produced them, idle decorations of the scene. They are additional forces. They reconstruct. They open new avenues of endeavor and impose new labors. In short they are civilization, culture, morality.[3]

2. Alasdair MacIntyre, *After Virtue*, 2d ed. (Notre Dame, Ind.: University of Notre Dame Press, 1984), pp. 189–90.

3. John Dewey, *Human Nature and Conduct* (1922) in *John Dewey: The Middle Works, 1899–1924*, vol. 14, ed. Jo Ann Boydston (Carbondale: Southern Illinois University Press, 1983), p. 57.

The history of a particular human activity, including the knowledge necessary to practice the activity, and the history of the development of its purposes and its governing norms is one and the same history. Social changes create new needs and interests, and people are spurred to seek new techniques to fulfill those interests. Discoveries in the area of technique suggest new possibilities, and changes in techniques and purposes effect changes in the norms in accordance with which the activity is done well or badly. Such developments, of course, are influenced by the larger social context, which may decisively affect practitioners' and clients' interests, capabilities, and resources. The effects of the development of an activity may in important ways alter "the common life." The norms and purposes associated with the activity, however, are every bit as much creations of human practical intelligence as the activity itself. Activity, purpose, and norms are interrelated in such a way that an understanding of any one of them requires an understanding of the others.

2

The proposal is to view morality as a body of practical knowledge, a social artifact that has resulted from what people have learned over time from their efforts to cope with certain practical problems encountered in the course of their lives. There is, of course, a great deal of resistance to this idea. To claim that morality is a cultural artifact is to espouse some form of ethical relativism. It strikes many people that the importance and authority of moral considerations cannot be accounted for on such a view. The notion that morality is a human creation that changes through time implies, it is thought, that morality is somehow arbitrary. The view is thought to depreciate morality. The sources of these objections are deep and complex, but it is clear at the outset that there is a defense against them. Some of the things that are generally acknowledged to be bodies of practical knowledge that are human creations are clearly of the first importance; consider such things as medicine, scientific inquiry, agriculture, liberal education—or choose your own examples. It is not plausible, moreover, to say of all such bodies of practical knowledge that they are objectionably arbitrary or that the standards that these bodies offer to govern practice are without authority. The importance of a particular body of practical knowledge is a matter to be determined by people's needs and what they can do with the knowledge. A body of knowledge that enables them to pursue successfully important needs and interests is unlikely to be objectionably arbitrary. If we understand and appreciate properly the importance of a particular body of practical knowledge, the standards that knowledge offers to govern practice will not lack for proper authority. A body of practical knowledge, then, can be important, well founded, and authoritative, whatever its origin. The thesis that morality is a body of practical knowledge that has been developed slowly and painfully by people over time is not incompatible with the claim that morality is important, well-founded, and authoritative. On this view, its importance is determined by considering what interests of ours it serves and how effectively it serves those interests.

3

There is a difference between morality and such paradigmatic bodies of practical knowledge as medicine, navigation, scientific inquiry, and music—a difference that raises immediate doubts about whether the former should be classified with the latter. Medicine pertains to the activity of healing, navigation to finding one's way, and music to the activity of making music. To what area of human activity does morality pertain? Of what do we have knowledge, what do we know how to do, when we absorb the body of practical knowledge called morality? Similar reflections led certain ancient Greeks to note that there were no generally recognized experts in virtue and to debate whether virtue could be taught.

Moral considerations can be relevant to a broad range of different activities, for presumably morality in some way or other governs all our activities. It is knowledge we all need, whatever our specialized tasks may be, whatever our circumstances. It is knowledge of how to live. So, we might say, as medicine is the body of practical knowledge that pertains to the activity of healing, so morality is the practical knowledge that pertains to the activity of living. It seems strange, though, to suppose that *living* is an activity on all fours with healing, finding one's way at sea, making music, and so forth. The activity of living to a considerable extent *consists in* such things as making music and healing people. It is not something else we do *in addition* to these things. Why, then, in order to live, do we need to have practical knowledge of anything more than the specific activities that make up our lives?

The practical knowledge we call morality is, in a way, an important part of our practical knowledge of the specific activities that constitute our lives. It is not something separate from the knowledge of specific activities. Knowledge of moral considerations is entangled with knowledge of how to pursue specific activities. One could not first learn how to discharge the roles of scientific inquirer, family member, citizen, and friend and then subsequently learn about honesty, loyalty, unselfishness, trustworthiness, and restraint. On the other hand, morality is more general in the scope of its application than specific technical practical knowledge; it pertains to a great many activities. Its domain comprises many different activities, whereas medicine pertains to the activity of healing, agriculture to raising food, and so on.

Morality, moreover, is more internally heterogeneous than these paradigmatic bodies of practical knowledge. It is not focused upon one particular sort of interest or purpose as navigation or agriculture is. It is a hodge-podge of ways of acting, ways that arise from our struggle with a great many different sorts of problems we encounter in the course of engaging in a variety of different activities in a social context. Its similarity to other kinds of practical knowledge is clearer when we focus on the elements in this collection. Compared with music or navigation, morality is a disjointed body of knowledge—hardly a body at all. Morality, then, is a heterogeneous collection of various items of practical knowledge that pertain to a variety of different activities, rather than a knowledge of how to do one separate thing called living.

Human social life is complex; there is a division of labor that requires people to master special sorts of practical knowledge that pertain to their specific kinds of work. Thus we have medicine, music, politics, and many other fields. All of these activities are social, however, and the community is the arena in which people together pursue these specialized activities. The very existence of these specialized activities requires a community with shared notions of what ends to pursue and how to pursue them. Communities are of various kinds with various purposes, such as families, neighborhoods, and political states. The knowledge of how properly to fulfill any of several roles in such communities is an area of practical knowledge too. In the pursuit of their work and in the fulfillment of their roles in various communities, problems arise for people, collectively and as individuals, concerning such matters as agreement, cooperation, and coordination. Knowing how to deal with these and other problems that are concerned with the peculiarly social character of human life and activity is properly characterized as practical knowledge. In fact, these problems arise in many different ways, and the methods people have developed for resolving them are multifarious. We have come to denote these ways of resolving problems of living together, or some not very clearly defined subset of these ways, by the term "morality." Medicine, navigation, and music are bodies of knowledge, each one of which pertains to a variety of subactivities; think of the variety of things embraced by music. Each of these bodies of knowledge is homogeneous, however, in comparison with the variety of ways of dealing with problems that constitutes morality.

It is perhaps misleading to conceive of morality as a *body* of practical knowledge in the sense that medicine is a body. For more than one reason, we select from among the norms that govern various practical domains, various areas of life and activity, certain norms that are found in more than one domain. We place these together—on a list of Ten Commandments, for example. Placing them on a list in this way does not produce a body of practical knowledge; they remain a list of disparate items of practical knowledge extracted from the domains that give them their meaning. This point is important.

4

We resist the suggestion that morality is a hodge-podge. We seek unity and system in ethics. If there is not a single principle such as the Categorical Imperative or the General Happiness Principle from which all other moral principles are derived, then there must at least be a relatively small number of fundamental principles from which the rest derive, perhaps as theorems derive from a consistent set of axioms in mathematics. The results of these assumptions in ethical theory are not impressive, and the failure of these theories is at least partly explained by the Procrustean nature of these attempts to impose unity and system upon what is neither a unit nor a system.[4]

Suppose someone were to claim that the whole of our technical practical knowledge can be systematized in such a way that every part of it is derivable from the same relatively small number of fundamental items of practical knowledge. This would mean that the knowledge required to practice all of the arts, crafts, and professions would be contained in this one system. The system would embrace sculpture, medicine, agriculture, violin making, and so on. We would at the outset have serious doubts about this claim. For one thing, the characteristic purposes of the various arts and professions are very different, and the practical knowledge proper to each activity is substantially knowledge of how to achieve its characteristic purpose. It is possible, of course, to maintain that the purpose of every art and profession is the same: they are all meant to serve our needs and interests, to satisfy our desires. That the same general description can be applied to the purpose of every art, however, does not make all arts into a single body of practical knowledge. In fact a mastery of one art is not likely to be necessary or sufficient for mastery of another. Aristotle made the point , in criticism of Plato, that there is no single science of "the good."[5] Similarly, there is not one single practical science of serving needs and interests or satisfying desires. If one wants to understand the technical practical knowledge we do have, it is necessary to consider separately the particular ways that have been developed to achieve a variety of different results.

Instead of seeking an illuminating way to view all fields of technical knowledge as means of pursuing a single common purpose,

4. Perhaps the most sustained discussion of various attempts to systematize morality, together with acute criticism of these attempts, is found in Henry Sidgwick, *The Methods of Ethics*, 7th ed. (London: Macmillan, 1907). I reconstruct Sidgwick's discussion in *Moral Relevance and Moral Conflict* (Ithaca: Cornell University Press, 1988), chap. 2.
5. *Nicomachean Ethics*, 1, 6, 1096a 30–34.

we might accept the variety of common purposes and seek to reduce the number of principles for pursuing these purposes to a relatively small number. The study of particular areas of practical knowledge involved in this program might result in an understanding of those pursuits, but it is not at all clear that the attempt to weave the materials abstracted from these fields into a single system would contribute appreciably to the understanding of these practices. The "system" would remain a disjointed collection of accounts of importantly different areas of practical knowledge.

The similarities and differences between this imaginary project that attempts to combine all technical knowledge into one system and the project of moral theorizing are suggestive. The phenomena that moral theorists theorize about are heterogeneous. Moral theorists are concerned with how to act with respect to such matters as agreements, cooperation, reciprocity, trust, property, role responsibilities, authority, and so on. They consider the bearing upon practical questions of such considerations as life, truth, compassion, honor, loyalty, friendship, justice, and so forth. An understanding and appreciation of the ways in which considerations of friendship and loyalty affect conduct does not suffice for knowing how to proceed in matters involving property or authority. Friendship, on the one hand, and property, on the other, are altogether different matters. If one wants to learn about them, one must study two different subject matters. A difficult practical problem about friendship requires that one think about the large and complex subject of relationships among people based upon their caring about one another, while a problem about property requires that one reflect upon an equally complex but different subject.

If you are faced with such a difficult practical problem, and I tell you to satisfy as many of the most important desires as possible, this is not likely to be helpful advice. It is of the same order of usefulness as the advice, "Do what you should do." There are descriptions that apply to the aims of serious individuals whenever they struggle with a moral problem: 'doing what should be done,' 'doing what is best,' for example. This does not render the practical knowledge that constitutes morality a single practical subject, any more than describing the aims of all the arts as satisfying desires renders the arts a single system.

If we think of morality as consisting of practical knowledge, it appears to be a hodge-podge of ways of dealing with a great many different sorts of issues and problems that arise for people as they engage in a variety of different activities. So far the program of moral theorizing, conceived as weaving all moral knowledge into a single system, is no more inviting or promising than the imaginary project of systematizing all technical knowledge.

5

Why, then, has systematic moral theorizing seemed not only feasible but important, whereas there is no interest in the systematization of technical knowledge? However misguided these theoretical efforts are, the impulse to make consistent our ways of coping with pressing practical issues is of the first importance in understanding practical reasoning. A very prominent feature of the moral dimension of our existence is the conflict of practical considerations. We continually encounter situations in which one consideration indicates strongly that we do one thing and another consideration indicates strongly that we do a contrary thing. Such conflicts are very common in our experience, and some of the most difficult practical problems take this form. In attempting to resolve conflict problems, we are engaged in the effort to make our store of practical knowledge more consistent, more harmonious. This harmonizing is not done, however, by manipulating formulae in the abstract; rather it is done in the context of concrete practical problems, where a solution of the concrete problem often has the effect that one or more of the conflicting moral considerations gets modified by a plan that attempts in some way to take both considerations into account.[6] Once again, the concrete situation is absolutely central.

6. Frederick L. Will calls this "the mutant-producing capacity of problematic subsumption." For a general discussion of this phenomenon in many areas of reasoning see his *Beyond Deduction: Ampliative Aspects of Philosophical Reflection* (New York: Routledge, 1988), especially chap. 5. John Dewey described this form of deliberation in *Human Nature and Conduct*, chap. 16. I develop an example of such a resolution of a conflict of moral considerations in *Moral Relevance and Moral Conflict*, chap. 3.

Utilitarianism, on the one hand, and natural law theories and other absolutist conceptions, on the other, all in one way or another deny the reality of conflict problems. The view that morality is a collection of diverse items of practical knowledge of very wide and general application across practical domains explains why conflict problems should be so common. This is a version of the thesis that Berlin called pluralism. The view also points to an explanation of how such problems might be resolved. On the latter view, moral considerations are associated with learned ways of dealing with certain sorts of difficulties that are encountered in the pursuit of various interests in a multitude of practical domains. Such considerations have a point or purpose that derives from the role that they play in our various activities, from the needs and interests served by the ways with which the considerations are associated. In this Heraclitian world, there frequently arise novel situations that bring considerations into conflict in more or less unprecedented ways. Such problems are properly resolved, when they are resolvable at all, by reflecting upon the points of the considerations involved. The aim is first to adapt considerations where necessary to unprecedented situations by altering the considerations so as to preserve their points as far as possible while enabling people to get on with the activity at hand. It is also important that the alterations contemplated may impact upon life in other practical domains, so another very general aim is to disrupt other areas of life as little as possible. The best outcome is to discover modifications that, while satisfying the above conditions, in addition positively reinforce other important practical considerations, and so advance the activities themselves and the possibility of their pursuit together with other important activities. That there sometimes are such solutions is a fact. There may be conflict problems, however, that do not admit of any very satisfactory resolution.

I am claiming that *general* considerations are involved in these problems and that their solution often involves adapting and modifying such considerations. I am talking here about general considerations such as truthfulness and seriousness about one's undertakings. When some individual undertakes to serve as an advocate—defending someone in a court of law, selling automobiles for a dealer, or presenting an academic department's needs to the university administration—these two general considerations, truthfulness and doing what one has undertaken to do, are apt to come into conflict. Let us say, cautiously, that these considerations are principles. We are considering cases in which important moral principles come into conflict. We obviously cannot give up either of these general principles. Think what truthfulness means generally in human life, in such areas as scientific research, teaching, family life, political activities, friendships, commerce, and courts of law. Think, too, of what is at stake in one's responsibilities to those whom one has undertaken to serve as an advocate. What one should do in concrete situations in which such considerations conflict, I claim, is to seek a way to modify the principles in such a way that (1) one can observe them both, (2) the roles, that is, the purposes of the principles in the activity at hand are preserved, and (3) the modification occasions a minimum of disruption elsewhere.

For example, one might think about adopting the idea that one's responsibility to one's advocatees is to defend their rights and interests within the limits of scrupulous truthfulness. Suppose, though, that one's legal client has told one in confidence that he was previously convicted of an offense similar to the one with which he is currently charged. The presiding judge asks one if the client has ever been convicted of such a crime. The circumstances are such that one's refusal to answer the question will be taken by the judge to imply an affirmative answer to the question. One might well decide that one should lie to the judge, especially if the question is an improper one and a truthful answer will harm the client. This alternative is preferable to a strict adherence to truthfulness, which will result in a failure to protect fully the client's rights in the circumstances.[7] This may involve a modification of one's view of a legal advocate's responsibility to be truthful. Later efforts to proceed with this modified conception may reveal that it is inadequate.

How can anyone defend lying? This is the reaction of a decent person who is not attending to all aspects of the problem. It is helpful to respond to the question with another question: How can anyone defend an advocate's allowing her client's rights to be violated

7. For a discussion of the problem of how an attorney is to respond to such an improper question from a judge, see Kenneth Kipnis, *Legal Ethics* (Englewood Cliffs, N.J.: Prentice Hall, 1966), pp. 94–95.

when she could prevent it? The fact is that both considerations are involved, and the two considerations conflict. It no more solves the dilemma to point out that lying is immoral than it does to point out that injustice and not fulfilling one's undertakings are immoral. Conflicts such as this one are ubiquitous, and the most common error that people make in struggling with these problems is to seize upon one consideration, proclaim it sacred and inviolable, and ignore the other considerations. The positions people take on all sides of the abortion controversy provide examples of this mistake.

There is a powerful intellectual temptation to suppose that morality consists in a body of principles or rules that unambiguously indicate the right thing to do in every circumstance. To yield to this temptation, however, would be to ignore our experience; it is evident that no such clear directions are available to us. One sort of moral theorizing consists in seeking a way to discern such a body of absolute principles behind the moral knowledge individuals actually have and employ, assuming that if existing resources can be clarified and systematized, the result will be a body of knowledge that unambiguously indicates what should be done in every conceivable circumstance, a set of principles so structured that no conflicts can arise between them. Unfortunately, there is more than one way in which the Ten Commandments or the morality we learn at our parents' knees can be clarified and systematized, and the question arises, how would one be able to tell which systematization is the one that invariably indicates the right actions? This is a most unpromising program, and the results are what one would expect.[8]

We know we should be truthful, and we know that we should fulfill our undertakings. We cannot say with any confidence, however, that when these principles conflict, truthfulness is always more important than one's commitments, or vice versa. Yet in some particular situations where these considerations conflict, it is clear as can be that one is more important than the other. This suggests to some that we are able to discern, on a case-by-case basis, how conflicts are properly resolved, even though we have no general principles to guide us in resolving conflicts. One form of intuitionistic moral phi-

---

8. On this point, see Arthur E. Murphy, *The Theory of Practical Reason* (LaSalle, Ill.: Open Court, 1964), pp. 116–18.

losophy recognizes a variety of moral considerations or principles that frequently conflict with one another but denies that there are general considerations or principles that govern the proper resolution of such conflicts. On W. D. Ross's version of this view, serious people are simply able to discern the proper resolution of conflicts in particular cases—they see which consideration is most important.[9] On such a view, we know such general truths as, for example, "One ought to be truthful" and "One ought to fulfill one's undertakings," but this knowledge comes to nothing more than knowing, respectively, that there is reason to be truthful and there is reason to honor one's commitments. It is evident that, on this conception, the general knowledge embodied in moral principles can play no useful role in resolving conflicts between these principles. On the supposition that there are objectively better or worse solutions to conflict problems, proponents of this view conclude that one intuits the superior solution without the guidance of general knowledge.

We may well wonder what the difference is on this view between intuiting in a particular conflict problem that one consideration is more important than another and arbitrarily declaring that one consideration is more important. Embracing this form of ethical intuitionism is an act of desperation. It is important to note too that the minimalist account this view offers of what one knows when one understands a moral principle or a moral consideration is most implausible. If all I know about truth-telling as a practical consideration is that we have a reason to tell the truth, I do not understand about truth-telling. The sort of practical knowledge that moral agents have when they know about truth-telling as a moral consideration, when they understand the principle that they should tell the truth, consists in a great deal more than just the knowledge that they have a reason to tell the truth. One has a fuller or lesser knowledge and understanding of truth-telling as a practical consideration depending upon the extent of one's understanding of the importance of truth *in various areas of life,* why it is important, and how it is to be compared in importance with other considerations that pertain in these areas. A corollary of this last claim is that one cannot understand a consideration such as truthfulness in isolation. One must un-

9. W. D. Ross, *The Right and the Good* (Oxford: Clarendon Press, 1930), chap. 2.

derstand one consideration in conjunction with other considerations; understanding a practical consideration involves understanding one or more activities or practices.

6

Suppose, for example, that as a child, one first learns about the importance of truthfulness in family contexts where it plays a role in nurturing, protecting, and educating. What one has learned has applications to commerce, government, mature friendships, scholarship, courts of law, and poker, but the lessons require modification and extension to adapt them to these different activities and to the different mixes of considerations that operate together with truthfulness in these areas. These adaptations need not be compromises in the sense of corruptions. When one moves from the context of family to a court of law or to business, new and different considerations of an order of importance comparable to truthfulness come into play. The application of the consideration of truthfulness must be modified in order that other crucial considerations may have their run. The task of modification and adjustment of moral considerations is never completed, since the activities to which they are relevant continually undergo change.

Vincent, a defense attorney, is generally truthful, but when he defends a client in court, he sometimes on behalf of his client says things he does not believe. Defense attorneys are sometimes criticized for aiding and abetting lying when they enter a plea of not guilty at the request of a client who has confessed guilt to them in confidence. Should the client subsequently take the witness stand as the defendant in a criminal trial and, in response to the attorney's questioning, tell a story the attorney knows to be false, the attorney is criticized for being an accomplice in perjury. If the lawyer then goes on to argue in defense of the client, citing the perjured testimony in making his case, the lawyer is, according to the critic, not only an accomplice in another's lies, but is actually asserting those lies to the court.

Suppose Vincent, outside of court, is apparently a truthful person, with the appropriate attitude toward the considerations that indicate when the truth should be told. In a criminal trial, however, Vincent will sometimes knowingly assist a client to plead and testify falsely, and he will build upon such testimony in arguing the case. Is he thereby violating the norms of truthfulness? One important purpose of a criminal trial is that the truth be found so that justice can be done. At the same time, when clients confess their guilt to their attorneys in confidence, the attorneys have an obligation to protect those confidences. Since every accused individual has a right to a fair trial, and competent legal counsel is necessary for a fair trial, it is not clear that attorneys should withdraw when faced with this problem.

A lawyer in such a situation is involved in a conflict of moral considerations, caught between role responsibility and duty to client on the one hand, and the claims of truth and retributive justice on the other. Some commentators—Sissela Bok, for example—claim that attorneys who build in this way on their client's testimony which they know to be perjured thereby fail to tell the truth when they should.[10] On the other hand, it can be argued, as Monroe Freedman and Kenneth Kipnis do, that defense attorneys may be doing exactly what they should do when they build on their client's perjured testimony in a criminal proceeding.[11] Unless Vincent is sworn as a witness, Kipnis would argue, his statements in arguing before the court are not testimony, not evidence to be considered with other evidence. Rather, the attorney points out how the evidence admitted can be construed in a way that is as favorable as possible to his client. It is the responsibility of judges and juries to decide about the credibility of the testimony of a witness and other evidence submitted. In performing their role, it is not necessarily wrong for defense attorneys to cite the testimony of witnesses and point out what the testimony implies, even though they do not themselves find the evidence credible. Attorneys' beliefs are not germane, and it would be wrong for them to inject their beliefs into a trial, unless they are also testifying as witnesses.

Lawyers, however, have a legal and professional responsibility not to make statements they know to be false to a tribunal and not to

10. Sissela Bok, *Lying: Moral Choice in Public and Private Life* (New York: Random House, 1979), pp. 166–73.

11. Monroe H. Freedman, *Lawyers' Ethics in an Adversary System* (Indianapolis, Ind.: Bobbs-Merrill, 1975), pp. 27–42, and Kipnis, *Legal Ethics*, chap. 5, pp. 80–95.

offer any evidence they know to be false.[12] At the same time, they have a responsibility to protect the confidences of their clients. When the attorney's client is the accused in a criminal proceeding, and the client's testimony is known by the attorney to be perjurious, then these duties conflict with one another. Bok argues that the duty of confidentiality to clients is actually a practice adopted by lawyers for their own purposes, a practice that could not survive informed public scrutiny when it was used to justify complicity in perjury.[13]

Kipnis argues, in response to Bok, that the practice of attorney-client confidentiality plays an indispensable role in securing an accused person's right to a fair trial. For important reasons, we think that every accused person should have counsel, due process, the right to present evidence, and the right to cross-examine witnesses. These and other important rights can be secured only if the accused has skilled legal assistance. It is the defense lawyer's responsibility to advise and assist the client in order to secure these rights. To do this, the attorney must learn from the client the pertinent facts, but clients will not be forthcoming with these facts unless they are assured that their revelations will be kept in confidence. Kipnis argues that an understanding that clients must not tell their lawyers of facts that imply their guilt will substantially interfere with the attorneys' ability to advise them properly. Lawyers must be able to guarantee confidentiality in order properly to perform their work as defense attorneys.

Here is Freedman on these points:

First, the lawyer is required to determine "all relevant facts known to the accused", because "counsel cannot properly perform their duties without knowing the truth". The lawyer who is ignorant of any potentially relevant fact "incapacitates himself to serve his client effectively", because "an adequate defense cannot be framed if the lawyer does not know what is likely to develop at trial". (27)

If we recognize that professional responsibility requires that an advocate have full knowledge of every pertinent fact, then the

12. See Rule 3.3 of the American Bar Association Model Code, which can be found in Rena A. Gorlin, ed., *Codes of Professional Responsibility*, 2d ed. (Washington, D.C.: Bureau of National Affairs, 1990), pp. 365–68.
13. Bok, *Lying*, pp. 162–64.

lawyer must seek the truth from the client, not shun it. That means that the attorney will have to dig and pry and cajole, and, even then, the lawyer will not be successful without convincing the client that full disclosure to the lawyer will never result in prejudice to the client by any word or action of the attorney. This is particularly true in the case of the indigent defendant, who meets the lawyer for the first time in the cell block or the rotunda of the jail. . . . It is no easy task to persuade that client to talk freely without fear of harm. (30)[14]

If, therefore, a client accused of a crime announces the intention to commit perjury on the witness stand, the attorney must inform the client of the seriousness of that offense. If the client persists, the attorney must either withdraw or proceed to question the client on the witness stand in the usual way and treat the testimony in the usual way in arguing the case. The practice of lawyers' withdrawing in such circumstances will result either in clients' eventually learning to keep important information from their attorneys or in clients' inability to secure proper counsel.

This is what is at stake in attorney-client confidentiality. What, however, shows that it is more important to protect confidentiality than to reveal perjury to the court? A strong argument would be one that succeeded in showing that, all things considered, the important aims of a criminal trial were better served by protecting confidences in these circumstances than by requiring attorneys to report their clients' perjury. Suppose attorneys generally report their clients' perjury in these circumstances, and this fact is generally known. If this practice had the consequence that clients kept incriminating facts from their attorneys, then so far the aims of a trial would not be advanced. Attorneys would not be able to report perjury if they did not know of it, and attorneys would be hampered in their efforts to advise their clients effectively by their lack of pertinent knowledge. So, generally, this practice would not advance the cause of the emergence of the truth in a criminal trial, and it would interfere with a

14. Freedman, *Lawyers' Ethics in an Adversary System*. (I have omitted Freedman's references in these passages.) Freedman offers examples of the ways in which a client's withholding information from the attorney can defeat the latter's efforts to provide necessary legal advice. See pages 30–32.

defense lawyer's ability to elicit information from the client that the lawyer needs in order to protect the client's rights and provide informed counsel. On the other hand, if attorneys generally built on their clients' perjured testimony in these circumstances, and this were generally known, judges and juries would have to determine the credibility of such testimony independently of the attorney's behavior. It does not seem to me at all implausible to think that the practice of criminal trials would go better if attorneys proceeded in these cases as Freedman and Kipnis recommend and questioned their clients on the stand in the normal way when they knew them to be lying. That is, the practice would be better in the sense of more effectively accomplishing the aims of criminal law. If this is right, then the argument indicates a way of harmonizing the respect for truth with attorney-client confidentiality in the conduct of defense lawyers in a certain sort of situation. Attorneys would continue to be obligated to refrain from offering evidence they know to be false. If they know the testimony of a collateral witness to be false, they would be obligated to report that matter. They would be obligated to advise their clients against offering perjured testimony. Where clients who are defendants in criminal proceedings ignore this advice, and attorneys cannot report their perjury without revealing matters clients have told them in confidence, then attorneys should not treat their testimony in any way that would reveal confidential disclosures.[15]

Defense lawyers sometimes face a problem that involves a conflict between the important duty not to introduce false testimony or countenance perjury and the duty to respect and protect the confidences of clients. Rule 3.3 of the American Bar Association's Model Rules of Professional Conduct (1989) indicates that a lawyer should disclose perjury and refuse to enter false evidence even if this action breaches attorney-client confidentiality. In a comment on this rule, the authors of the code acknowledge that the proper solution to the

15. One reviewer of Freedman's book understands him to be defending attorneys' building on clients' perjured testimony on the basis of an absolutist view of confidentiality. Freedman's argument, though, does not need the premise that an attorney's duty to respect a client's confidences admits of no exceptions. See Ronald D. Rotunda, "Book Review: *Lawyers' Ethics in an Adversary System* by Monroe H. Freedman," *Harvard Law Review* 89 (January 1976), 622–33.

problem of the perjurious client in a *criminal* trial is a matter of controversy.[16] Whichever side is right in this argument, the point is that the resolution of the problem depends upon reconciling as far as possible important conflicting ethical considerations in a way that permits the several central purposes and values of the judicial system to be realized.

If Freedman and Kipnis are right, then within the complex body of moral and legal norms that govern the conduct of defense lawyers in a criminal trial, Vincent's building on perjured testimony by a client in a criminal trial is not a failure to tell the truth, or to respect the truth, when he should. If this conclusion is correct, then Vincent is doing what he should do, and his behavior does not count against his record of truthfulness. It does not exhibit a flaw in his character.

Notice here that the issue of whether Vincent's behavior exhibits a failure of integrity, a flaw in his character, turns upon the question whether in a certain kind of context individuals should avoid saying what they know to be false, which in turn requires attention to the complex of norms that pertain to conduct in those contexts. What those norms are and what they indicate may in some cases be unclear or controverted. If Vincent has a firm disposition to do what the appropriate norms indicate about saying what is true or false— whatever that might turn out to be—does that disposition, by itself, constitute the virtue truthfulness? I think not. If Vincent is sufficiently unclear quite generally about when he should tell the truth, his disposition to tell the truth when he should will be ineffective— it will not be a tendency to act as he should that results in his actually so acting. Vincent must also have a knowledge of *other* norms relevant to what he is doing and the ability to work out what action those norms *together* indicate. A virtue such as truthfulness involves very extensive practical knowledge.

A concern to tell the truth when he should, together with the ability to work out when he should tell the truth in those practical domains with which he is familiar, might reasonably be said to constitute the virtue, truthfulness, in Vincent. Note, though, that what Vincent is thereby disposed to do cannot be captured in some

---

16. See the "Comment" on Rule 3.3 of the American Bar Association Model Code (Gorlin, *Codes*, pp. 366–67). I am grateful to Nicholas Malfese for bringing this to my attention.

compact specific action-description such as 'saying what is true' or 'saying what is true except. . . .' Vincent's truthfulness involves, rather, an understanding of several highly complex domains of human activity, activities that are governed simultaneously by a body of norms that indicate the appropriate ways of acting in the domain, including when one should, all things considered, say only what one takes to be true. A court of law is such a domain, and the relevant norms that pertain to the activities therein are many and complexly interrelated. The plurality of norms and purposes invariably leads to conflicts among them. The emergence of truth in a trial is an important consideration, but it is only one of a number of important considerations. Individuals who are able to participate properly in a trial in any of several roles require a practical understanding of a highly complex activity, a mastery of the activity, which involves the ability to observe simultaneously a body of norms that often conflict. They must have an appreciation of the relative importance of a variety of aims and purposes, some internal to the activity. Such an appreciation is essential for being able to resolve conflicts among considerations in a way that responds as far as possible to all relevant considerations while still enabling individuals to pursue the activity. The good character that an individual exhibits in the role of a defense attorney involves a highly complex set of skills, competencies, appreciations, and valuings. Located in an individual, the structured set of understandings, appreciations, and competencies necessary for participating properly in one or more practical domains constitutes good character. The structure of the components of such a character—their relative unity and harmony—will reflect the structure of the activities in which that character is exhibited.

7

Violet is a child who is truthful. She has an understanding of the domains of the household, the school, and the playground, including a knowledge of when she should tell the truth in her activities in these domains. She has, in a sense, mastered the relevant bodies of practical knowledge. We do not normally think of the knowledge necessary in order to fulfill a child's role in a family or school as constituting a *body* of practical knowledge, but the knowledge Violet needs in her domains differs primarily in complexity from the knowledge Vincent needs to serve as a defense attorney. Violet's truthfulness will not be global in the sense that she, as serious as she is about doing what she should, can reasonably be expected, without further tuition, to act as she should with respect to truth-telling in *other* domains—as a salesperson, an advocate, a diplomat, or a poker player. The practical lessons that inculcated Violet with truthfulness will have to be supplemented by further learning about when she should tell the truth before she can be expected to act as she should with respect to speaking the truth in certain situations that arise in these unfamiliar domains. These lessons will have to include training in law, commerce, international relations, and card playing. In this respect, we are all more or less like Violet. Our practical knowledge as adults is apt to be wider than hers, because we have mastered more activities in more domains. There remain, however, for each of us, a great many relatively unfamiliar domains. When should an international diplomat tell the truth? A psychotherapist? A spouse in a polygamous marriage?

Truthful people cannot be expected always to exhibit their truthfulness effectively in unfamiliar practical domains, nor can unintelligent people be counted upon in familiar domains when things get complicated. This is not necessarily because the temptations to lie are stronger in unfamiliar domains or the commitment to truthfulness weaker. One's knowledge of when one should tell the truth is less secure in domains that one does not adequately understand. We know on reflection that there is more to the moral life than the struggle to make ourselves do what we know perfectly well we should do. There is also the struggle to work out what we should do. Philosophers, and psychologists, too, tend to forget that not all failures of decent people to do as they should do are the result of yielding to temptation.[17]

People who think seriously about ethics, whatever their disciplinary background, often fail to appreciate that practical norms pre-

---

17. The controversy among psychologists about whether character traits are "global" or "situation sensitive" is muddied by a failure to recognize this point. For a discussion of this controversy see Owen Flanagan, *Varieties of Moral Personality* (Cambridge: Harvard University Press, 1991), chap. 13.

---

sent themselves to us in clusters, the membership of the clusters being determined by the nature of the activities in which we are engaged and the larger social context in which the activity is pursued. We have to work out what the relevant norms *together* indicate about how we should proceed, taking account of all the things we are doing and all the purposes we have. This is what is going on in the attempt to determine whether it is appropriate for defense attorneys to build on perjured testimony. The mix of norms changes from domain to domain and even from circumstance to circumstance within domains. Activities themselves change and develop. Life and events perpetually move. The changing concrete situation is nearly everything in determining what we should do. Continual readjustments are necessary in order to give a moving cluster of norms their due as best we can.[18]

The fact that we follow groups of norms rather than single norms one at a time is overlooked when philosophers attempt to formulate, one at a time, clear and explicit exceptionless moral rules that will unfailingly tell us what we should do in every circumstance. Not surprisingly, the program encounters endless difficulties. Some philosophers, discouraged by the lack of success in this enterprise, find attractive the idea that what accounts for people's being morally good, to the extent that they are, is not the possession of rules, but rather the possession of good character traits, virtues. They adopt as a philosophical program the study of virtues, in the hope that they can answer important questions in ethics without becoming embroiled in the vexed problems encountered in trying to formulate exceptionless moral rules or other sorts of algorithms for right conduct. Of course, one cannot, by focusing on virtues, escape problems about understanding the norms that determine what we should do. Virtues are essentially tendencies to do what we should do, or at least to act well, in certain matters. Virtue ethics does not provide a theoretical end-run around the norms, including moral norms, that govern conduct.

It is a mistake to suppose that the virtue truthfulness acquired early in life can suffice for telling the truth as one should across all

18. The foregoing discussion is an application of Frederick L. Will's account of the role of a "composition" of norms of thought and action in critical assessment. See his *Beyond Deduction*, especially chap. 7.

the practical domains that one subsequently encounters. This mistaken notion, though, is suggestively similar to the idea that the rule, 'Always tell the truth, except . . . ,' with the exceptions spelled out explicitly, learned early on, is all one needs in order to be able to tell the truth as one should throughout one's life. Both mistakes overlook the point that we follow norms in groups, that the membership of the groups varies across domains of activity, and that the norms themselves are continually altered by our efforts to adjust our practice to novel circumstances. The apparent situation sensitivity of traits of good character is not entirely due to the moral weakness of our natures or to the liability of our goodness to come undone in the face of opposing inclinations.

The naive but curiously seductive idea, that in studying character traits we are concerned exclusively with phenomena internal to human beings, helps to support the notion that we can study virtues without becoming entangled with problems about external behavior and its norms. The structure of many, perhaps all, character traits is provided, to a very considerable extent, by the activities we are engaged in when we exhibit them—after all, the traits are substantially tendencies *to act*. Thinking of traits as internal phenomena that form an economic system or as forces that produce our actions is harmless as long as it is clear to us that these are metaphors. We need to keep firmly in mind that the way to study the traits that make up moral character is to study the lives and the activities of people who possess them. Philosophers and psychologists must continually remind themselves of the fact that character traits are not usefully conceived as phenomena hidden "inside" human beings. Primarily, we have men and women acting and reacting in the world. Internal to their activities are purposes and norms—values and standards of right and wrong ways of doing things. When they learn how to participate in these activities, then certain practical knowledge is "in" them—they make the norms and purposes of these activities their own to a greater and lesser extent, and they acquire the knowledge and skill to participate in the activities. The shape of their psychological dispositions concerning these activities is, to a considerable extent, provided by the activities themselves. Character traits are *relations* of certain kinds of individuals to a structured social environment, complex adjustments of individuals to forms of life that are elaborate and changing. Such dispositions (tendencies, habits) are for the most part acquired through interaction by individuals with the world; the history of individuals' interaction with the world and other people shapes them and the natural impulses they have, and an important aspect of the form they acquire thereby is their learned tendencies to act. To understand character traits so acquired, one must understand the life of the individuals, the activities they engage in when they acquire and exhibit the traits. The way to study character traits, as Aristotle knew well, is to study their full actualization, the acts that express them.

8

The psychologist Stanley Milgram's studies of obedience are widely taken to show that it is disturbingly easy to devise circumstances in which decent people will act badly.[19] The subjects in Milgram's experiments were told that their task was to serve as "teachers" in an investigation of the effects of punishment on learning. The teachers were directed to ask questions of learners and to apply an electric shock to the learners when they gave the wrong answer. After each shock, the voltage was to be turned up a step, so the shocks were progressively more severe. Teachers and learners were told that although the shocks would eventually become very painful, they would not cause any tissue damage. The teacher-subjects thought that the learners were volunteer subjects like themselves, but actually the learners were in cahoots with the experimenter. The learners gave wrong answers with some frequency, and they gave convincing performances of being in increasingly severe agony when the teacher-subjects pressed dummy shock buttons. When teacher-subjects expressed concern about the severity of the pain the "learners" were apparently undergoing, they were told firmly by the experimenter that they must continue. Milgram found

19. Stanley Milgram, "Behavioral Study of Obedience," *Journal of Abnormal and Social Psychology* 67.4 (1963), 371–78. These experiments and the various controversies they have provoked are described in Arthur G. Miller, *The Obedience Experiments* (New York: Praeger, 1986). See also Bok, *Lying,* chap. 13, and Flanagan, *Varieties of Moral Personality,* chap. 14.

that 65 percent of the subjects would continue to administer what they thought were increasingly painful shocks until they reached the end of the experiment and the experimenter gave them permission to stop.

It is quite generally thought that the results of Milgram's studies show that, in Hannah Arendt's words about Adolf Eichmann, "in certain circumstances the most ordinary decent person can become a criminal." Such circumstances "cause ordinary traits to come undone," or "cause people to reveal that they lack a trait we expected them to have," or "they expose the limited range of a disposition—for example, compassion—which we thought had wider scope."[20]

I am far from convinced that the 65 percent of the subjects who kept on shocking the "learners" to the end of the experiment for that reason acted badly, or that they thereby failed to show compassion when they should. If one looks at the problem from the standpoint of the deceived subject, it is not at all clear what he should do when the learner screams and protests upon being shocked. Of course, one should avoid hurting people. Both teacher-subject and learner, however, undertook to participate in this experiment, on the understanding that the learner would likely experience repeated and ever-more-severe pain. That the teacher-subject is causing the learner severe pain is not the only moral consideration in this situation. The teacher-subject has a straightforward contractual obligation to the investigator, and has good reason to believe that the learner does too. The psychologist has entangled the subject in an acute moral conflict; as the infliction of pain becomes more disturbing and disagreeable, the investigator firmly reminds the subject of his commitment to see it through. Notice that the investigator's only authority here is based upon the subject's prior commitment to take part in the study and to accept the investigator's directions. The subject must resolve this moral conflict, but its proper resolution is unclear. The learner, too, is apparently bound by a commitment to see things through, in the knowledge that this will involve enduring some severe pain. In these days of institutional review boards, the rule is that a subject may withdraw from an experiment at any time, but there was no such understanding in Milgram's laboratory in the 1960s. The investigator

20. Flanagan, *Varieties of Moral Personality*, p. 293.

has provided mixed signals concerning the learner's safety—on the one hand assurances from a distinguished scientist that the shock will not do physical harm, on the other, "danger" warnings on the teacher-subject's voltage control panel. The situation from the subject's standpoint is a moral muddle in the midst of ambiguities. And it is a nasty muddle at that: Milgram reported of the subjects that "in a large number of cases the degree of tension reached extremes that are rarely seen in sociopsychological laboratory studies."[21]

To ensure that subjects would not know anything about "obedience experiments," Milgram sought men who were not connected with academia.[22] One consequence of this was that these individuals were likely to be unfamiliar with psychological research, laboratories, and the role of experimental subjects. Their lack of familiarity with their situation, combined with their inability to judge for themselves the importance of completing the experiment and the consequences for the study of their refusing to complete it, must have made it very difficult for them to judge whether they should continue to hurt the learner or withdraw.

One critic of Milgram's treatment of his experimental subjects pointed out that a volunteer subject in a laboratory, like a patient in a clinic, reasonably expects help and protection from professionals: "The laboratory is unfamiliar as a setting and the rules of behavior ambiguous compared to a clinician's office. Because of the anxiety and passivity generated by the setting, the subject is more prone to behave in an obedient, suggestible manner in the laboratory than elsewhere. . . . The baseline for these phenomena as found in the laboratory is probably much higher than in most other settings."[23] The ordinary compassionate person, unfamiliar with psychology experiments and laboratories, is in a very poor position to resolve the difficult moral conflict Milgram created for him. The claim that 65 percent of Milgram's subjects acted *badly* is open to serious doubt.

21. Milgram, "Behavioral Study of Obedience," p. 375. Diana Baumrind criticized Milgram's treatment of his volunteer subjects, expressing skepticism about his claim that the harm of the extreme stress they underwent was adequately dissipated by "dehoaxing" and reassurances that they had not actually hurt anyone. See her "Some Thoughts on Ethics of Research: After Reading Milgram's 'Behavioral Study of Obedience'," *American Psychologist* 19 (1964), 421–23.
22. Miller, *The Obedience Experiments*, p. 38.
23. Baumrind, "Some Thoughts on Ethics of Research," p. 421.

The plausibility of Milgram's account of what his studies showed depends upon our focusing upon a single consideration, avoiding causing pain, and a single trait, compassion. The teacher-subject's continuing to shock the learner is assumed to be a departure from compassion and ordinary decency. The behavior is viewed as resulting from the subject's slavish deference to authority. Milgram suggested that he had uncovered something very sinister in these studies—the very psychological phenomenon that led "good" Germans to participate in the crimes of the Holocaust.

The apparent pain of the learner resulting from the "shocks" is not the only morally relevant consideration from the perspective of the teacher-subjects. The subjects reasonably believed that they and the learners had made a commitment to take part in an important scientific study under the direction of a capable experimental psychologist. Their problem was to determine whether the suffering of the learner and the learner's protests canceled the original agreements to take part in a scientific study, and unfamiliarity with experiments and inability to determine for themselves the consequences for the study of their refusal to continue seriously compromised their ability to decide the matter. How does Milgram miss this, and how does he induce others to overlook this point? He focuses upon what he thinks of as the situation sensitivity of the trait, compassion. When compassion is not expressed in the subject's behavior in the most direct manner by a refusal to continue to shock the learner, Milgram assumes that he has an instance of the "situation sensitivity," the quirkiness of the subject's compassion. Compassion is a moral virtue, so this instance of situation sensitivity is immediately assumed to be an instance of moral failure, of the undoing of ordinary compassion. Milgram's mistake is not due simply to the intellectual habits peculiar to experimental psychologists. Seizing upon a single consideration in a morally complex situation while ignoring other relevant considerations is a very common error in practical reasoning and assessment.

A better description of the teacher-subject's problem when the learner cries out and begs to withdraw is this: How am I to harmonize the dictates of compassion with the other norms that pertain to the behavior of a volunteer in this sort of psychological experiment? The teacher-subject's continuing to act in a way that distresses the learner may be no more a failure of ordinary compassion than the

actions of a teacher who gives a student a low grade for poor work
or a hiring officer who declines to appoint an unqualified job applicant. Of course, Milgram's assumption from the outset that the situation of the teacher-subject is in all morally relevant respects like the
situation of individuals ordered to take part in the wholesale murder of innocent people tends to obscure the actual character of the
teacher-subject's problem.

9

The starting point in practical philosophy is the existing practical
domains, consisting of activities and practices that are social and
historical artifacts. Associated with these activities and interrelated
with them are norms and characteristic purposes. Practitioners learn
to follow the norms that are multiple and likely to conflict. A general
problem, then, in mastering any complex activity is learning to observe simultaneously the many pertinent norms, and the solution of
this recurring problem requires modifying and adjusting the norms
so that they can be observed together. Where the context in which
the activity takes place is changing, the project of adjustment is
never completed.

Most activities, however they differ one from another, involve cooperation among participants, coordination, and communication. It
is not surprising, then, that certain norms tend to recur from domain
to domain. People live in communities where individuals and
groups pursue various activities in close proximity with one another. There are complex interrelations among the activities that are
pursued in a community. Norms in one domain will reflect the necessity of pursuing its activity in such a way that activities in other
domains can be pursued. Certain of the norms that are of general
relevance and importance across practical domains are for one reason or another noted and placed together on a list. This is what we
call morality. The particular group of norms that comprise morality,
however, are not associated as a group with any particular activity
or body of practical knowledge. They are not, as such, a group of
norms that people attempt to observe all together in the course of
mastering and participating in a particular activity. Thus, these

norms are not related to one another as are the norms that together guide people in the practice of a particular activity such as medicine, family life, or politics. The latter norms are more or less adjusted to one another so that they can be simultaneously pursued. The norms that comprise morality, however, because they do not together govern a particular practice, are not so adjusted to one another. Their adjustment comes when they are observed in the pursuit of a particular activity, when they are adjusted to all of the other norms that pertain to the pursuit of that particular activity. It is the particular activity that structures the norms; the norms on the list that comprises morality are in that respect unstructured in their relation to one another.

Understanding any particular norm is a matter of understanding how it contributes to a practice, what its importance is in the practice, and how it can be observed together with other norms that pertain in the particular practice. One can say general things about lying that are of use in dealing with concrete problems that arise across many domains, but how the norms of truthfulness will apply in a particular domain—say, when practitioners are confronted with a particular problem—will depend decisively on the nature of the activity, its purposes, and its norms, including the other pertinent moral norms. Ethics is not an autonomous practical science that can be mastered independently of the particular complex activities that constitute the larger life.

While morality is not itself a body of practical knowledge, in the sense that agriculture or architecture is, it is intimately bound up with such bodies of knowledge. Morality refers to practical considerations, principles, norms that apply to more than one practical domain—considerations that are important in many activities. Moral norms, however, get their point and authority from the various activities to which they belong. Understanding such a consideration is a matter of understanding its role in various practical domains, where it, together with a great many other practical considerations, guides our practice. The meaning of a moral principle is given by its role in combination with other considerations in guiding the activity in one or more practical domains.

Much of what I have said about norms of morality would seem to be true as well of what might be called norms of rationality. How do the latter differ from the former? Norms of rationality, like moral norms, apply quite generally across many practical domains to such things as agriculture, navigation, medicine, and building, as well as to theorizing. Norms of rationality, however, pertain particularly to activities that can be called in a broad sense, *inquiry*—seeking answers to questions, calculating, deliberating, and reasoning. The norms of rationality are ways of proceeding well in inquiry—ways that reliably lead to appropriate answers, decisions, and conclusions. Inquiry in this very general sense, itself an activity, is an important component or accompaniment of all human activities. The sorts of inquiry called for in one activity may differ from that appropriate to another activity, but finding the answers to questions is everywhere important. The norms that govern inquiry in its various forms, norms of rationality, are thus important in all domains, including practical domains. The results of successfully following these norms, rational beliefs and acts, are typically to be found in all domains. Being good at deliberating about the conduct of life, as Aristotle saw, is both a virtue of character and a virtue of thought, an excellence of an inquirer. If one deliberates well about a matter of moral importance, one's decision (one's answer to the question, What shall I do?) is apt to be reasonable and the action decided upon is apt to be morally appropriate. Some norms of inquiry are also moral norms. Moral norms, however, unlike norms of rationality, do not pertain *particularly* to the component of inquiry in activities. The norms of rationality are more like the norms of music or medicine in that they form a body structured by a particular activity. Moral norms, as a group, are not focused upon a particular kind of activity. Norms of rationality guide us specifically in inquiry; there is no one activity to which the norms of morality are specific.

3. Norms as Instruments

> Norms are bound together, though with greatly various degrees of tightness: bound together as instruments, vehicles for producing in thought and action what in large spheres of life are counted as *ways* of life; of professions, crafts; modes of cultural enjoyment, modes of ethical and religious cultivation and devotion.
>
> —Frederick L. Will, "Philosophic Governance of Norms"

1

In his 1920 book, *Reconstruction in Philosophy*, John Dewey maintained that important changes in intellectual practices and outlook that make the twentieth century view of the world so different from that of people just a few centuries ago have bypassed moral philosophy altogether.[1] These changes, according to Dewey, have been very fruitful; it is detrimental to philosophical ethics that they have not penetrated there. The notion that in "physical inquiry," we properly begin with universal conceptions and subsume particular cases under them came to be rejected when people realized that such a procedure "confirmed prejudices and sanctioned ideas that had gained currency irrespective of evidence for them; while [i.e., whereas, by contrast] placing the initial and final weight upon the

---

1. John Dewey, *Reconstruction in Philosophy*, in *John Dewey: The Middle Works, 1899–1924*, vol. 12, chap. 7. Unless otherwise indicated, numbers in parentheses in the text refer to pages in this edition.

individual case, stimulated painstaking inquiry into facts and examination of principles" (174). This intellectual epiphany, applied to ethics, would "transfer . . . the burden of the moral life from following rules or pursuing fixed ends over to the detection of the ills that need remedy in a special case and the formation of plans and methods for dealing with them" (174). "Ethical theory ever since [the Greeks] has been singularly hypnotized by the notion that its business is to discover some final end or good or some ultimate and supreme law" (172).

Despite deep disagreements among moral philosophers influenced by natural law theory, or Kant, or utilitarianism, these philosophers tend to share the assumptions that at the center of ethics is some fixed purpose or eternal unchanging law, and that it is their task to find it. Dewey challenged these assumptions. The application to ethics of the ways of thinking that have been so fruitful in other areas, Dewey said, would require that we believe "in a plurality of changing, moving, individualized goods and ends" and that we conceive of principles, standards, and laws as "intellectual instruments for analyzing individual or unique situations" (173).

It is morally and intellectually stultifying to proceed upon the assumption that moral principles are fixed and unchangeable. Philosophical ethics began with the Greeks, Dewey said, as an attempt to find regulation for the conduct of life that has a basis in purpose instead of resting upon blind obedience to custom. The aim of the enterprise was to free people from rigid practical requirements imposed upon them from the outside so that they are free to use their understanding and knowledge to direct their lives intelligently. The attempt to accomplish this purpose by discovering unchanging rules or ends and following them or pursuing them no matter what, would, if successful, defeat the original purpose of ethics. The assumption that goods, ends, and moral principles are fixed—are eternal or unchanging—Dewey suggested, is a holdover from earlier times when social organizations themselves were regarded as permanently fixed in a certain form—feudal times, for example. It goes with a belief in an ordered cosmos in which rest is "higher" than motion (172). The philosophical view that there is a deep epistemological separation between fact and value, so that ways of thinking about matters of fact are not appropriate to the latter, is an additional support for the assumption that we must think about morals differently from the ways that we think about "factual matters."

Dewey's recommendation that the particular practical problem be made the center of attention in understanding moral norms is not meant to deny the importance of norms in resolving the problems. The norms are viewed as instruments whose proper role is as aids in dealing with the particular case. Like any good tool, the norms are to be understood by reference to the function they actually perform, and the locus of this performance is the particular, concrete practical problem. The origin and development of practical norms, including moral norms, is to be found in the particular problems that have been resolved with their help.

When moral norms are conceived as Dewey suggests, as "intellectual instruments" to be used in dealing with concrete problems, it is very natural to assume that such norms are open to modification—that their modification is sometimes desirable. Generally, we profit from the attitude that our instruments can be improved and that we can learn how to improve them from our experience in using them in particular situations. "Growth," according to Dewey, is "the only moral 'end' " (181).

2

Dewey's account of moral norms as intellectual instruments that get their character from the particular cases in which they are employed is congruent with the view of ethics and practical knowledge explained in the preceding chapter. Truthfulness or compassion, as moral considerations, typically will pertain to a variety of practical domains, but understanding such a practical consideration involves understanding how it is to be taken into account together with other pertinent considerations in one or more activities. Such understanding is a matter of knowing how to apply the consideration to a range of particular cases. Our experience with particular situations will have shown us that a certain regard for the truth or for the flourishing of our neighbors contributes in specific ways to life in particular practical domains. This knowledge is a help, a tool, in resolving new practical problems that involve concerns about truth or neighbors' welfare.

Someone who has a well-developed and sophisticated understanding of truthfulness as a moral consideration, however, does not
have the body of unambiguous moral instructions envisioned by the
moral absolutist; no one goes into real situations with all of the possible practical moral problems already resolved. People do have
general principles, however—items of practical knowledge that
have figured prominently in the solution of past problems. This
knowledge involves an understanding of why these considerations
matter and an appreciation of what is at stake in these things. In
other words, one has intellectual tools and experience in their use,
and these promise the ability to solve the next problem, if one has
sufficient ingenuity and persistence. So, Dewey said:

> Morals is not a catalogue of acts nor a set of rules to be applied like
> drugstore prescriptions or cook-book recipes. The need in morals is
> for specific methods of inquiry and of contrivance: Methods of in-
> quiry to locate difficulties and evils; methods of contrivance to
> form plans to be used as working hypotheses in dealing with them.
> And the pragmatic import of the logic of individualized situations,
> each having its own irreplaceable good and principle, is to transfer
> the attention of theory from preoccupation with general concep-
> tions to the problem of developing effective methods of inquiry.
> (177)

If one resolves a problem in a certain way, and the solution can
qualify as a good one, it will be possible to give an account of the
matter that explains why the solution is adequate. The account will
take the form of showing that in the course of pursuing a certain
kind of activity in a certain social context, taking account of its purposes and its relation to other activities, it is appropriate under certain circumstances to proceed in such and such a way. The account
will be general. It is apt to be longer than what we think of as a formulation of a principle, but it contains the claim that it would be
appropriate in the future to proceed in the way described in sufficiently similar cases. The substance of this account may constitute a
new item of practical knowledge in the sense that it constitutes a revision, a re-forming of old items of knowledge. The new practical
knowledge is then available to use in the future, where it is apt to be

further revised in response to new circumstances. It is important that it be possible to give such an account of why we proceed as we do, for otherwise we cannot show that we have not proceeded arbitrarily or capriciously. Ethical intuitionism—the view that implies that we properly resolve conflicts between moral considerations by seeing that one is more important than the other in a particular case, without there being any possibility of giving a general account of the matter—is unsatisfactory for this reason. It must be possible in general to distinguish between a reasoned, intelligent solution to a practical problem and an arbitrary choice.

In routine sorts of problems, we may be able to make a case for a solution by citing an already existing, well-established principle or policy that dictates a certain solution. There will be unprecedented practical problems, however, for which we have no satisfactory policy—problems where no existing principle is clearly applicable or where relevant considerations dictate contrary courses of action. In such cases, we must make policies or principles to deal with the problem. Such principles, however, are not created from nothing, nor need we, as a rule, choose arbitrarily among possible alternatives. The policies must respond to the particular needs presented by the concrete problem. The particular problem will give us people's initial purposes and some barrier to the activity that normally satisfies those purposes. There will be ways of dealing with more or less analogous situations, and we must consider whether these ways can be adapted to the problem at hand and at what cost. Principles in conflict will have one or more points, and our interest in and concern with these points will remain. We seek a solution which in the circumstances answers, as far as possible, to the interests at stake in all considerations or which does the least damage to those interests. We seek ways to realize the points of all considerations without compromising their effectiveness and with as little disruption and damage as possible to other important concerns. We seek to take the knowledge we already have and reorganize it in such a way that it can be brought to bear fruitfully on the unprecedented problem.

The shared learned ways, the items of practical knowledge that comprise morality, then, are various; they serve a variety of purposes. Novel situations presenting unprecedented problems challenge this knowledge, and the appropriate response is reorganization and adaptation. The procedure here is improvisational, and ingenuity is an important virtue. Even if the positive morality is relatively harmonious and adequate at one particular time, the next problems a changing world presents are apt to be ones people are not prepared for. If they are intelligent and resourceful enough to adapt their ways to solve novel problems and to deal with the conflicts that such adaptations may engender, then they grow, they progress. This, I take it, is the sort of growth that Dewey called the "only moral end."[2] Whether this happens, however, depends upon the richness of their practical knowledge, their ingenuity and courage, and the difficulty of the problems. Nothing guarantees progress. In applying moral considerations to real problems, however, we are often engaged in the process of changing morality and altering the way that activities are conceived and pursued.

3

In discussing legal reasoning in hard cases, Ronald Dworkin employs an example that illustrates the way that carefully reasoned applications of practical considerations in a particular case can alter the considerations.[3] The relevant norm is not a moral norm, but the example is transparent and suggestive of matters that merit pursuit. A rule of a chess tournament provides that the referee shall declare a game forfeit if one player unreasonably annoys the other in the course of play. During a game, the Russian grandmaster Tal continually smiles at his opponent Fischer in such a way as to unnerve him. Fischer complains that he is being unreasonably annoyed. Does the rule apply here? Is it relevant in this case? It is important in deciding this question, Dworkin says, to consider the character of the game of chess. "Given that chess is an intellectual game, is it, like poker, intellectual in some sense that includes ability at psychological intimidation? Or is it, like mathematics, intellectual in some

2. John Dewey describes this process of growth in several works. See, for example, *Art as Experience* (1934), in *John Dewey: The Later Works, 1925–1953* (Carbondale: Southern Illinois University Press, 1989), vol. 10, chap. 1.
3. Ronald Dworkin, *Taking Rights Seriously* (Cambridge: Harvard University Press, 1977), pp. 101–5.

sense that does not include that ability? . . . Given that chess is an intellectual game of some sort, what follows about reasonable behavior in a chess game? Is ability at psychological intimidation, or ability to resist such intimidation, really an intellectual quality?" (103).

When it is unclear to us whether a certain practical consideration applies in a particular case, we need to look closely at the point of the consideration. In Dworkin's example, the consideration in question, the norm, is a rule that pertains to a game. The point of this rule, presumably, is to preserve the character of the game of chess. The rule is an instrument, an *intellectual* instrument, designed to perform some function that serves this purpose. The rule pretty clearly prohibits players from such distracting behavior as making loud noises or repeatedly touching their opponents. The rationale for prohibiting this is that the outcome of a chess match should be determined by players' strategic and analytic skills, and such skills can be exercised only when players are able to concentrate. Players do need other qualities—such as endurance and a certain ability to concentrate. If, however, the game were regularly played under circumstances in which endurance regularly triumphed over intellectual ability—if, for example, players had no opportunity to rest during prolonged matches—then the game of chess would be changed in ways that would make it a quite different and probably less interesting game. Similarly, if players were permitted to shout and pummel one another during play, then the ability to think in chaotic circumstances would become as important in chess as the reasoning skills, and again the resulting game would be different and less interesting. The rule prohibiting players from "unreasonably annoying" one another is meant to preserve in such ways the character of chess as an "intellectual game" by ruling out behavior by players that interferes with the exercise of intellectual skills and that prevent such skills from being decisive in the conduct of play.

Dworkin's example involves a circumstance that raises the question of whether the sort of psychological intimidation Tal attempts here is consistent with the kind of intellectual contest that chess is. This question may be one that has not been considered before, but Tal's behavior and Fischer's protest raise the question, and it needs to be settled. How we understand the rule in question—what we take "unreasonable annoyance" to mean—will be affected by the decision in this case. As a result of the decision, the rule will have been changed. The rule will be determinate in a way that it was not before the decision. Our understanding of the point of this rule will also be altered—made more determinate in a certain respect—and so too will be our understanding of the game of chess. This will be equally true whether the decision is that the rule is relevant in this case or that it is not relevant.

This example, of course, concerns the determination of the applicability of a game rule. Game rules are not the same as moral considerations, and the domain of games rules is different from many other practical domains. Games such as chess have explicit rules and relatively formal procedures for applying them. Games, moreover, are in a way compartmentalized; it is less usual for the resolution of problems about the application of game rules to affect substantially practice in other areas of life. Other domains, where moral issues tend to be of greater moment, are both less formalized and less compartmentalized than chess. Dworkin offered the chess example to illustrate a point about how hard cases are properly adjudicated in law. There are, though, important similarities between the reasonable application of practical considerations in games, in the law, and in the conduct of life generally.[4]

It is clear in Dworkin's example that in order to be able to discuss the question of whether it is consistent with the character of chess to permit psychological intimidation such as Tal's, one needs to have an understanding of a certain social practice—the game of chess. What the game actually is and what interests it serves will be central in determining how the rule prohibiting unreasonable annoyance is applied. The rule itself is an instrument devised to prevent certain sorts of interference that threaten to hinder the sort of play that chess players appreciate and cultivate. I have maintained that in order to apply certain practical considerations that pertain to the conduct of life generally, one needs to understand some of the activities which comprise people's lives. The proper resolution of difficult practical problems, including moral ones, requires us to ap-

4. For an extended discussion of how the solution of a particular moral problem requires the modification of a moral consideration, see my *Moral Relevance and Moral Conflict*, chap. 5.

peal to the character of existing social practice, and the facts about such activities will be important determinants of how these problems are properly resolved. To understand a particular moral consideration, one must understand how it together with other practical considerations applies to a range of activities and what the points of the various considerations are in their applications to these activities, and one must understand the activities themselves.

4

Do people, in fact, properly modify moral considerations in the course of applying them to difficult problems? It used to be thought that lending money at interest is a wicked practice, a clear instance of injustice. Now, however, in Europe and America, charging a fair rate of interest for loans is generally thought to be reasonable and proper. How did this change come about? In their book *The Abuse of Casuistry*, Albert Jonsen and Stephen Toulmin describe the movement in Europe from the view that charging *any* interest for loans of money—"usury"—is a particularly reprehensible form of robbery and hence wrong, to the view that it is generally appropriate to charge interest for money lent, as long as the interest charged is not excessive.[5] This change in the moral assessment of lending money at interest took place gradually over centuries, but it represents a substantial change.

As Jonsen and Toulmin describe it, the change of moral view was connected with the gradual realization that social conditions had changed, creating circumstances in society so different from the ones that had occasioned the earlier prohibition of lending at interest that the old idea that charging interest was always stealing was no longer plausible.

A 'loan' was understood as assistance to someone in need or distress. In the subsistence economies that existed from the time of the

5. Albert R. Jonsen and Stephen Toulmin, *The Abuse of Casuistry: A History of Moral Reasoning* (Berkeley and Los Angeles: University of California Press, 1988). Unless otherwise indicated, numbers in parentheses in the text refer to pages of this book.

writing of Deuteronomy up through the early Middle Ages, the failure of a crop or the loss of a flock could threaten the life of a poor man and his family; and the loan of seed, of a ewe for breeding, or of food might be lifesaving. In such circumstances, to demand 'more than was given' would clearly be exploitation of one's 'brother' or neighbor. While loans were certainly given in other circumstances, the paradigm for the moral analysis of usury appears to have been aid in time of distress. (183)

The moral case against usury in earlier times was this: People should help their neighbors in times of difficulty, and help in the form of lending needed money or goods is an important form of assistance. The owner may stipulate that the principal is to be returned; so much may be justified. There is not a justification, however, for demanding that more than the principal lent is to be returned. The lender is not giving up to the borrower anything of value beyond the principal; no labor is being done by the lender. A borrower in desperate need of a loan might agree to repay more than the principal borrowed, but this would be simply because of desperation. The lender who insists upon a promise to repay more than the principal is exploiting the borrower's desperate situation, coercing the borrower into giving up property to which the lender has no claim. The case is similar to the way that robbers or kidnappers coerce their victims to part with property, except that the usurist is an extortionist of opportunity. In economic circumstances where idle money and goods are just that, where the practice of investing in hopes of a return is not a readily available option, the paradigm of theft by opportunistic extortion generally fit well the activity of lending money at interest.

Theologians and canonists from the twelfth and thirteenth centuries argued on this basis that lending money at interest is absolutely morally impermissible (183–84). At the same time, partnerships where one party supplied the money and took a share of the profits from the venture were regarded as different from usury. Where one partner supplies a ship and sails it while the other partner supplies money to buy a cargo, the latter is entitled, if the venture is successful, to a return of the principal plus a share of the profits. The canonists, however, did not view this as a loan. The financier does not transfer ownership of the money to the captain, and any profit or loss from the venture is shared by the partners. This activity did not fall under the prohibition of usury.

> Aquinas developed the argument: one who commits his money to a joint enterprise does not give up its ownership; he takes the risk of its loss should the enterprise fail. He can take part of the profit that comes from the enterprise because it comes from his own property. Both partners are joint owners; both bear any losses and enjoy any profits. . . . The crucial moral difference between loan and *societas* [partnership] rested on the sharing of risk. By introducing the concept of risk as a modality in the argument, the first step toward a revision of the paradigm was taken. (185)

With great improvements in transportation and communication beginning in the fifteenth century, many new markets opened up. Burgeoning nation-states fought wars continually, and rulers sought money to finance them. There was an enormous demand for capital, and there were corresponding opportunities for investment (187). Political and mercantile entrepreneurs were eager for capital, yet for them to offer to pay for the use of others' money was apparently to invite others to commit the sin of usury. Convoluted financial arrangements were developed, these transactions having aspects at once of investment, insurance, and lending at interest. These were apparently intended in their complexity to provide banking houses with a wealth of reasons for denying that they were engaging in usury. In the sixteenth century, serious moralists debated for seventy-five years whether such financial practices were objectionable, until they gradually came to understand the special character of commercial loans (189–91).

Gradually, painfully, moralists came to see that the practice of lending money at interest in a mercantile context, where money itself had become a commodity and princes and entrepreneurs were eager for capital to fund their ventures, was different from lending idle surplus to a desperately needy neighbor. In a certain sort of community with a subsistence economy and little in the way of manufacture and trade, lending money at interest will tend to conform to the paradigm of taking advantage of neighbors' troubles and extorting from them profit to which the lenders have no just claim. When commerce and industry create a demand for accumulations of capital, the stage is set for lending at interest being desirable from the standpoint of both borrower and lender. The ideas that the lender extorts interest from the borrower and that the lender has no entitlement to the interest lose their plausibility. Even the loan to the desperate neighbor in trouble takes on a different aspect in this regard: the lender loses the opportunity to invest the principle during the term of the loan to the neighbor, and thus the lender has a claim to be compensated for this loss by charging interest.

Here then is an account of an historical change in moral ideas. The change is not simply a matter of moralists' caving in to demands of rulers, prelates, and bankers; it is not a corruption. Changes in political and economic circumstances required changes in the way that lending money at interest was viewed. On the other hand, this change was not a matter of discovering that people in the early Middle Ages were mistaken in thinking that usury was wrong. The understanding of property, money, and lending in early medieval times, grounded in their peculiar economic circumstances and practices, was different from ours, but sufficiently similar to current notions that we can with some effort understand these ideas. We can understand why in those earlier circumstances, lending at interest was regarded as stealing. The case for regarding lending at interest as theft makes sense in those circumstances. In fifteenth-century Europe, it made much less sense, and by the end of the sixteenth century, this was generally recognized.

What, exactly, was changed? The principle that lending money at interest is wrong was given up. Notions of when someone is entitled to compensation changed. In a way, what was understood by theft had changed, and the meaning of the principle that stealing is wrong changed. In another way, though, certain basic moral notions remained the same. Society and commerce are what changed, and these changed in such a way that the extortionate, the exploitative aspect of lending at interest was attenuated to a considerable degree. People wanted to borrow money and were eager to offer to pay interest as an incentive to lenders. The justification of such lending could be and was made in terms of existing notions of what entitled someone to compensation—"profit ceasing" and "loss incurring" (187–88). What happened, in fact, was this: People took moral notions and applied them to novel social circumstances in such a way that important new needs could be met, while retaining at the same time, in somewhat altered forms, moral considerations which they could not give up— charity to neighbors and entitlements to property.

This sort of continuity in change is an important aspect of successful solution of unprecedented practical problems, and the change of ideas about lending and usury represents a success. It is difficult for us, I suspect, properly to appreciate from our historical perspective the difficulty of this problem for Europeans in the sixteenth century and the magnitude of their achievement in solving it. It is clear to us now that loans at interest are not necessarily evil, but this could not be clear to people in that earlier time. They successfully adapted important moral ideas to these new circumstances that they only gradually came to understand; they removed social barriers to important new activities and ventures in ways that were largely consistent with their understanding of entitlement and charity. They accomplished this by gradually, painfully, coming to understand that prohibiting lending at interest in certain new circumstances did not serve the important purpose that the norm served in earlier times. Although they would not have described the development in these terms, they became aware of the prohibition against lending at interest as an instrument with a certain purpose, a purpose that was not served by using the instrument in its old form in certain novel circumstances.

The casuists of sixteenth-century Europe did not discover a previously existing principle that said there generally is such a thing as a fair rate of interest on a loan. Such a principle could not have existed in Europe in the Middle Ages, before there was a market for money and a circumstance where any idle capital was wanted for investment. The casuists did not create this principle from nothing, either. It is a reasoned adaptation to changed economic circumstances of ideas about what entitles individuals to compensation, an adaptation that is consistent with an important conception of charity toward one's neighbors. It is the continuity of the changed ideas with the earlier moral notions that prevents the change from being a corruption; the moralists of the fifteenth and sixteenth centuries were not being pragmatic in the vulgar sense. The instrumental conception of moral norms associated with philosophical pragmatism is not pragmatic in this vulgar sense that implies ignoring important moral norms.

Adherents to the view that moral norms remain fixed, eternal, and unchanging will be inclined to identify the moral in this account of the history of lending at interest with what remained constant—certain ideas about entitlement and charity. Of course, if a proper adaptation of moral considerations to unprecedented circumstances and problems requires continuity with previous norms, there will be some aspects of substantive moral notions that remain the same in every such change. There will be a great many other historical developments that involve these and other norms, however, and there is no reason to think that the particular aspects of morality that remained unchanged in the history of lending will remain unchanged in other such developments. In fact, it is apt to be the character and circumstances of the unprecedented problem that dictate what alterations will respond to the particular problem.

The search for morality in the form of a core of norms that remain unchanged in all historical examples of such adaptation is apt to lead to a retreat to ever more abstract and general formulations. Such precepts are not of much use in coping intelligently with the actual vicissitudes of human life; their abstractness and generality entail a lack of specificity that offers little guidance in particular circumstances. Theorists may not always realize this, because they tend to understand their abstract formulations in the light of their own current moral ideas. Michael Walzer remarks of the objective moral truths that some philosophers claim to discover in nature: "Most often, the moral principles here delivered to us are already in our possession, incorporated, as it were, long ago, familiar and well-thumbed by now. Philosophical discovery is likely to fall short of the radical newness and sharp specificity of divine revelation. Accounts of natural law or natural rights rarely ring true as descriptions of a new moral world."[6]

In response to the claim that no sane person could deny the principle that one should not be indifferent to the pain of one's neighbor, Walzer says,

6. Michael Walzer, *Interpretation and Social Criticism* (Cambridge: Harvard University Press, 1987), p. 6.

'Don't be indifferent' is not at all the same thing as 'Love thy neigh-bor as thyself.' And the second of these is unlikely to figure in the list of philosophical discoveries—if only because the question, Why should I love him *that much*? is not crazy. The principle of nonin-difference, or more positively, the principle of minimal concern, is conceivably a critical principle, but its strength is uncertain. A great deal of work would have to be done . . . to work out its relation to everyday social practice.[7]

The working out of the relation of a particular norm to everyday social practice involves understanding how its observance con-tributes to the pursuit of one or more activities together with an un-derstanding of how the particular norm can be observed in conjunction with a host of other norms that are implicit in the par-ticular context. How much weight one should give the pain of one's neighbor and what this indicates one should do will be very consid-erably affected by what other norms pertain and what these indi-cate. It is the particular social situation that determines which norms pertain.

5

My account of the relationship of particular cases to ethical con-siderations closely parallels Jonsen and Toulmin's account of the re-lationship of paradigm cases to ethical principles. Their paradigms are concrete cases that exemplify the application of principles in such a way that an important problem is solved. The paradigm case instances and exemplifies the successful use of one or more norms. It serves as a reminder of the proper employment of an intellectual instrument. When we encounter an unprecedented problem, where we have no paradigm, we search for various paradigms that repre-sent solutions to problems that are more or less like our novel prob-lem. The paradigms we find are an important resource for developing a new paradigm that pertains to our novel problem, but the existing paradigms may point in several directions at once. What

7. Ibid., pp. 8–9.

determines which existing paradigm, when adapted to our new problem, yields the best solution, all things considered?

One critic of Jonsen and Toulmin makes the following objection.

> The casuists' account of case analysis fails to supply us with principles of relevance that explain what binds the cases together and how the meaning of one case points beyond itself toward the resolution of subsequent cases. The casuist obviously cannot do without such principles of relevance; they are a necessary condition of any kind of moral taxonomy. Without principles of relevance, the cases would fly apart in all directions, rendering coherent speech, thought, and action about them impossible.[8]

What this objection says, in other words, is this: If we lack ethical principles that always provide clear and unambiguous directions for action when such direction is needed, then we must have other principles that clearly and unambiguously indicate how we are to apply the vague and incomplete ethical principles we do have. Otherwise, rational thought can offer no help in deciding what we should do in hard cases. Either we have principles that in the end tell us what to do, or principles offer no guidance.

In fact, there are neither ethical principles nor principles of relevance that clearly and unambiguously tell us what to do in hard cases. Fortunately, though, we are able to reason about hard cases without any such principles. The view behind the slogan that ethical principles are intellectual instruments is of help in seeing how this can be.

Consider a contemporary example that is not simple, but which, I think, represents a relatively successful completion of this sort of task. In the last several decades, we have seen the development of ever more effective medical lifesaving techniques that can be used to prolong the lives of individuals who are dying. Increasingly, this is possible with individuals who are severely and irreversibly incapacitated or damaged. For the first time, we are confronted with a great many situations in which the question arises, should medical people use these techniques to prolong the lives of such individuals? A consensus has developed that the right answer is sometimes "no."

8. John D. Arras, "Getting Down to Cases: The Revival of Casuistry in Bioethics," *Journal of Medicine and Philosophy* 16 (1991), 40.

People worry, for good reasons, that these medical means will be used to impose upon them an unwanted and burdensome extension of their lives in the form of a painful prolongation of their dying.

The development of powerful new life-prolonging techniques coincides with increasing concern on the part of medical patients to have a meaningful say in their own treatment—to exercise control over their own medical treatment. An educated, sophisticated class of patients, confronting physicians who are often relative strangers to them, demand to be full partners in decisions about their own medical treatment. An existing legal doctrine of "informed consent" is transformed into a requirement that physicians secure patients' consent to a treatment proposed after first telling patients, in terms patients can understand, what a reasonable person needs to know in order to make an intelligent decision in the matter.[9] It is understood that a mentally competent patient may decline a particular treatment and may withdraw from a course of treatment already begun.

A dying patient, then, may choose to refuse any or all life-prolonging treatments. This is an exercise of a patient's moral and legal prerogative. Such a decision, moreover, may well be in the patient's best interest. It can be a positive evil to an individual to have the process of dying prolonged. Both the principle of autonomy that mandates that patients retain important controls over the process of their medical treatment and the principle of beneficence that requires physicians vigorously to promote their patients' medical welfare indicate that lucid dying adult patients should be able to decline life-prolonging treatments and that their wishes should be respected. Here, then, is a paradigm that is of fairly recent development that is well established; the application of legal and ethical norms exemplified by this paradigm are accepted as appropriate. I will call this "the central paradigm."

There are, however, cases in which decisions must be made about using life-prolonging medical treatments with irreversibly damaged patients where the patient is not lucid, and, therefore, is unable to consent to or decline treatment. Such cases are significantly different from the central paradigm, but in certain of these cases, the solution

9. For a brief discussion with references of the evolution of this legal doctrine in the 1960s and 1970s, see Robert M. Veatch, *Case Studies in Medical Ethics* (Cambridge: Harvard University Press, 1977), pp. 304–6.

in the central paradigm is modified in the following way so that it suffices for the problem case. Where it is discovered that the incompetent patient previously indicated that he or she would not want life-prolonging medical treatment in circumstances such as the present one, then this is taken as the equivalent of the lucid patient's declining treatment in the central paradigm. This solution has evolved (and is evolving) through a series of widely discussed cases, including the famous legal cases of Karen Quinlin and Nancy Cruzan.[10]

Besides the central paradigm described above, there are other paradigms that suggest a different way of treating profoundly comatose dying patients. When a patient is brought to a hospital emergency room in need of emergency lifesaving treatment, and the patient is incapable of consenting to treatment, consent is presumed. Isn't this case more like the Quinlan case? The emergency room paradigm, itself settled and well-established, would suggest that we should presume that dying incompetent patients consent to lifesaving treatment. The central paradigm suggests one course of action with respect to the problem of the treatment of incompetent dying patients and the emergency room paradigm suggests a contrary one. What determines which paradigm should be decisive?

The answer to this question involves the serious contemporary concern that powerful lifesaving medical techniques not be used simply to prolong a burdensome life of poor quality in circumstances of catastrophic irreversible incapacitation and deterioration. People reasonably fear being in a circumstance where their incapacitation renders them unable to decline unwanted life-prolonging treatment. Skilled physicians are sometimes eager to use their newly acquired powers of treatment, even where the increment of life that is attained by these means is a burden to the patient. The device of the advance directive, the "living will" and durable power of attorney, promises to extend patients' control to circumstances where they are incapable of declining treatment. The adoption of the emergency room paradigm, on the other hand, would frustrate this con-

10. For a description and brief discussion of the Quinlan case, see Gregory E. Pence, *Classic Cases in Medical Ethics* (New York: McGraw-Hill, 1990), pp. 3–24. On the Cruzan case, see United States Supreme Court, *Cruzan v. Director, Missouri Dept. of Health*, U.S. 580 SLW 4916 (June 25, 1990), and Ronald Dworkin, "The Right to Death," *New York Review of Books*, January 31, 1991, 14–17.

cern. From the point of view of the patient's family and physician, if a patient has the prerogative of declining lifesaving treatment at the time it is offered, the prior directive serves a very similar function. Friends and family of the patient find it less painful to do as the patient has directed. It is preferable, then, all things considered, to adapt the way of proceeding in the central paradigm to the problem of the incompetent dying patient than to look to the emergency room paradigm. It is not hard and fast, transparent principles of relevance that indicate which paradigm is "most like" the problem case; it is the particular circumstances with the problems and concerns that are implicated in it that are decisive. So useful is this adaptation of the solution to the problem in the central paradigm to the case of the dying incompetent patient that we are all now urged to execute "living wills" and durable powers of attorney for health care. The compelling rationale for this advice is that, in the absence of an effective advance directive, the problem of how to treat the dying incompetent patient is much more difficult.[11]

Sometimes individuals who are not terminally ill, who with treatment would have a substantial period of life ahead of them, decline needed lifesaving treatment.[12] Then there are cases of seriously ill individuals who decline not medical treatment aimed at therapy but routine life-sustaining care—nourishment or hydration. These and other cases are more or less problematic to the extent that they differ in important ways from the central paradigm. It may aid in the solution of such cases to explore their similarities and differences to the paradigm. Of course, the case of the dying individual who asks to be killed immediately or who requests assistance in committing suicide differs enough from the central paradigm so that the use of the central paradigm in dealing with these cases is problematic.

It has, in fact, turned out to be very useful for solving certain of the problems in this area to view the problematic cases in relation to the settled central paradigm. For this purpose, the preceding has

11. During my three years of service on the Ethics Committee of a hospital, all of the cases brought to the committee for help involved questions about the treatment of dying, incompetent patients.

12. For a moving discussion of such a case see in Bette-Jane Crigger, ed., *Cases in Bioethics: Selections from the Hastings Center Report*, 2d ed. (New York: St. Martins Press, 1993), "A Demand To Die," pp. 118–22.

proved to be a better way of organizing the area of problems about the use of lifesaving medical treatment than the approach that takes "euthanasia" as the central paradigm in this area, and divides the cases into active and passive, voluntary and non-voluntary euthanasia. For one thing, the latter approach does not place a settled case at the center of the discussion.

There is a long-standing controversy, going back to the nineteenth century and beyond, that centers on the question of when it is morally justifiable for a physician to shorten the life of a dying patient. The dispute remains vexed and unresolved. The acceptance of the paradigm of the competent dying patient who has the prerogative of refusing lifesaving treatment is a relatively recent development. Not only does this address patients' worries about having their dying prolonged in an undesirable way, but it provides physicians with a solution to certain of their very difficult problems. Where the properly informed patient declines life-prolonging treatment, the question, "Can I justify proceeding in a way that shortens this patient's life?" does not arise for the physician. If the lucid, properly informed dying patient does not wish life-prolonging treatment, then this settles the matter. The physician's not treating the patient is then justified by appeal to the point that such a patient can be treated only with the patient's consent. This solution was sorely needed, because the development of medicine produced more and more instances of this problem.

The change in the controlling paradigm here represents satisfactory solutions to a range of difficult new problems. What has changed here and what remains the same? An obvious point is that medical technology created a variety of treatment options that did not exist before. It was assumed previously, moreover, that making the relevant choices of treatment was primarily the responsibility of the physician. The question of how physicians are to choose when some choices result in death for the patient was (and remains) vexed. Being responsible for another's death, choosing to let die rather than treat, heal, sustain, are obviously not things a physician can countenance lightly.[13] The new technology, however, proliferates

13. For a brief informed discussion of the problems of euthanasia and assisted suicide from the perspective of a physician, see Sherwin B. Nuland, *How We Die: Reflections on Life's Final Chapter* (New York: Alfred A. Knopf, 1994), chap. 7.

situations where decisions must be made about life-prolonging treatment. It is the conscious application to these cases of the principle that a physician must obtain the informed consent of a patient before undertaking treatment, with the understanding that the patient may decline any treatment proposed, that represents one important change. The principle itself underwent some modification in the process. A physician cannot treat a patient who refuses the treatment. Normally, the patient's refusal settles the matter. The problem is solved in a way that meets new needs by addressing patients' worries about their dying being prolonged and physicians' need for a way to deal with the proliferation of cases requiring decisions about the use of life-prolonging treatments with dying patients. The solution adopted preserves certain important considerations, while it modifies them. It is a limited but still very substantial success.

The American Medical Association, in a 1989 version of its "Principles of Medical Ethics," takes the following position on withholding or withdrawing life-prolonging medical treatment.

> The social commitment of the physician is to sustain life and relieve suffering. Where the performance of one duty conflicts with the other, the preferences of the patient should prevail. . . . For humane reasons, with informed consent, a physician may do what is medically necessary to alleviate severe pain, or cease or omit treatment to permit a terminally ill patient to die when death is imminent. However, the physician should not intentionally cause death.[14]

In response to an earlier version of this statement, one philosopher has accused the AMA of taking the untenable position that, while active euthanasia is morally impermissible for physicians, passive euthanasia for dying patients who want to die is justifiable. The criticism is that if it is wrong intentionally to bring about someone's death by doing something, it is equally wrong intentionally to bring about someone's death by *not* doing something.[15] As Bonnie Steinbock pointed out, the AMA is not taking the position that

14. "Principles of Medical Ethics and Current Opinions of the Council on Ethical and Judicial Affairs—1989," Section 2.20. This is found in Gorlin, *Codes*, p. 201.

15. See James Rachels, "Active and Passive Euthanasia," *New England Journal of Medicine* 292.2 (1975), 78–80.

physicians are justified in practicing passive euthanasia. Rather, the position is that where dying patients decline life-prolonging treatment, their wishes should prevail. Normally, there is no decision for physicians to make about whether or not to treat a patient who declines treatment.[16]

Many standard textbooks in medical ethics tend to misdescribe what has happened here. The issue of how to treat dying patients is discussed under the heading of "euthanasia," and this is not the way that most physicians view the matter presently, nor does the law treat this as a form of euthanasia or as physician-assisted suicide. Those latter issues remain unresolved; the solution to many problems involving how to treat dying patients has bypassed this dispute. This matter of the competent dying patient who declines life-prolonging treatment is settled, even though we have not, at the time of this writing, decided what to do about Dr. Kavorkian and his provision of assistance to people who want to commit suicide.

The change in ethical paradigms in the medical treatment of many dying patients from the unsettled paradigm of euthanasia to the paradigm of a patient's declining medical treatment is comparable to the historical development of the idea that it is legitimate to lend money at interest, providing that the interest is not "excessive." The latter development involved a change in the ethical paradigm of lending from helping a neighbor in desperate trouble at no cost to the lender to lending as an investment that often makes possible enterprises that require accumulations of capital.

An important aspect of the accounts we are considering is that the paradigm shifts described, which are the same thing as changes in moral norms and in activities, are not arbitrary, not arational, not without substantial justification. People took existing practical knowledge that did not contain explicit procedures for dealing with certain unprecedented problems, and re-formed it in the process of solving those problems. The solutions preserved portions of past settled practice that people were, for good reason, most reluctant to give up, while at the same time enabling them to pursue current interests, and respond to new concerns. The concrete problem was

---

16. Bonnie Steinbock, "The Intentional Termination of Life," *Ethics in Science and Medicine* 6.1 (1979), 59–64.

ever at the center. The kind of particularism that these developments are used to illustrate is not intuitionism; people can offer cogent arguments in defense of these solutions. The key is to view ethical norms as instruments developed in dealing with particular cases that are then modified to permit their application to novel cases.

4. Understanding Practices

Any casuistry that modestly restricts itself to interpreting and cataloguing the flickering shadows on the cave wall can easily be accused of lacking a critical edge.
—John Arras, "Getting Down to Cases"

1

An important objection needs to be considered at this point. The position I have been defending implies that our actual practice, in a way, determines what is right and wrong. This seems odd, because moral considerations, moral norms, are supposed to be the means for evaluating actual practice, the standards by which practice is judged. The particularist conception of practical reasoning set out in the preceding chapters makes practices judges in their own cases. Our existing practices and institutions, moreover, are in certain respects and to greater and lesser degrees unsatisfactory, imperfect. To the extent that such flawed artifacts influence the nature of the standards by which the artifacts themselves are judged, we are deprived of trustworthy means for the correction of flaws in practice. If we hold up a flawed practice to standards that are determined by the practice itself, this test cannot be trusted to reveal the flaws. Standards, then, should be independent of the matters they govern.[1]

1. Among the proponents of the necessity for norms to be independent of the matters they govern, Frederick Will lists Plato, Descartes, Augustine, and Dostoyevsky ("If God does not exist, then everything is permitted"). See "Philosophic Governance of Norms," pp. 345–46.

The idea that morality is a collection of items of practical knowledge and that the norms that comprise the collection are intellectual instruments for solving practical problems is useful in responding to this objection. The activities of chess players, physicians, and navigators are evaluated by standards that reflect the nature of their activity and the state of knowledge of the activity at the time. Such standards are by no means independent of the activities they govern. Practice in these areas is known to be imperfect in certain ways, yet the standards governing the practices function as standards. They are authoritative even though they are recognized as changeable and improvable. It is not true in general that effective standards by which activities are evaluated must be independent of those activities.

Nor is it true in general that if activities are flawed, and standards by which activities are judged are internal to activities themselves, then the flaws in the activities will not be apparent when the standards are applied to the activities. Inadequacies in our practical knowledge manifest themselves in many ways—most notably in our failures, or in "successes" purchased at exorbitant prices. When an activity regularly promises more than it actually delivers or when it is pursued at the cost of unacceptable disruptions elsewhere, these facts are available to critical participants. In a changing world, no body of practical knowledge can be said to be complete, nor can it be known to be adequate as it stands for any test it may have to face in the future. There are, moreover, obvious gaps in certain of these bodies of knowledge; there are certain problems we would like them to solve that they do not solve. We must allow for the possibility that certain of these inadequacies in our practical knowledge are due to false beliefs whose falsity we do not suspect. Some of these bodies of knowledge may be more adequate than others, and the same body of practical knowledge may be more adequate at one time than another. To note such inadequacies is perfectly compatible with noting the successes of these bodies of practical knowledge, and a true assessment of the adequacy of one of these bodies of knowledge at any time must take note of all these things, virtues and defects alike. A contempt for psychotherapy, for example, might show a failure to appreciate its successes and the difficulty of the problems it has failed to solve.

2

It is important to distinguish the objection that activities *cannot* in principle be evaluated effectively by standards internal to them from the objection that actual practice is in fact so thoroughly mistaken that any standards implicit in such practice are unworthy of our allegiance and respect. Those who view existing social practice as thoroughly stupid and corrupt will be disposed to reject whatever standards and values are implicit in such practice. In Plato's *Republic*, the character Thrasymachus maintains, in effect, that social morality is created by powerful manipulators in a community for the purpose of advancing their own selfish interests. These manipulators dupe the many into thinking that it is good for them to act in ways that actually benefit the manipulators at the expense of everyone else.[2] More modern philosophers, Nietzsche and Marx prominent among them, elaborate in complicated ways Thrasymachus's basic critique of morality. An additional objection, then, to a view that characterizes morality as norms that have developed in connection with actual practices is that such a view is vulnerable to the derogatory view of morality of Thrasymachus and his friends.

It is not necessary, however, for a proponent of the view that the social artifact we call morality is a collection of practical knowledge to accept claims such as Thrasymachus's about the character of morality. The incisiveness of certain of the social criticisms of a Marx or a Nietzsche does not establish their characterizations of morality generally. We can compare the relative merits of the Thrasymachus view of morality (or the views of Nietzsche or Marx) with the hypothesis that morality embodies a more or less adequate heterogeneous body of collective practical knowledge about how to deal with certain problems we have encountered in living with one another. Which hypothesis is better supported by the social facts? The facts about actual practice do not bear out the claim that morality is simply an engine of oppression of the ruling class or that it is nothing more than an invention of the mediocre herd to protect them-

2. Thrasymachus's position is stated in *Republic* 1. See especially 338c–339a and 343b–334c.

selves from superior people. The judgment that our actual practice, with its associated norms, is thoroughly mistaken and corrupt is no more plausible than the notion that it is flawless or perfect.

Error, self-deception, and hypocrisy are not uncommon in our experience, and we must be open to the possibility that we are mistaken about the character of a given practice or about its adequacy. When people approach some practical matter with a view of things based upon misunderstanding or fantasy, however, there are certain characteristic consequences—they frequently fail in what they attempt to do, or they find that their efforts interfere with other crucial things. This is complicated because we sometimes fail even when we have true beliefs and heretofore-adequate practical knowledge. We do, however, have ways of determining the causes of our failures. An existing social practice might be criticized for its failure to meet its own pretensions, for its internal conflicts, and by the standards implicit in other deeply held ways, including (other) moral ones. What the causes of these unsatisfactory conditions are and how they are to be remedied are matters to be determined by careful study of the actual practices and the concrete problems that exist. Regarding morality as a body of practical knowledge, then, does not prejudice the outcome of a study of morality in favor of a derogatory position such as Nietzsche's or Marx's.

In ancient Greek, *kalon* meant good, beautiful, *and* noble. This fact of language and whatever manipulations lay behind the fact, however, could not prevent Greeks from noticing that this trio of qualities did not always occur together. Certain highborn (i.e., noble) individuals they encountered were neither good nor beautiful. In Euripides' play *Electra* (written about 415 B.C.) the title character, a princess, has been forced to marry a peasant. The peasant treats her with kindness and respect, and Orestes, the brother of Electra, is impressed and grateful. Euripides has Orestes say,

> There's no clear sign to tell the quality of a man;
> Nature and place turn vice and virtue upside down.
> I've seen a noble father breed a worthless son,
> And good sons come of evil parents; a starved soul
> Housed in a rich man's palace, a great heart dressed in rags.
> By what sign, then, shall one tell good from bad?

. . . The best way
Is to judge each man as you find him; there's no rule.[3]

3

A difficult and important question arises here that must be for-
mulated and considered. I have maintained that practical reasoning
involves attempting to observe a number of norms simultaneously
in the context of pursuing one or more activities. The norms are
themselves thought to be plastic; the best solution to a practical difficulty will often require the modification of one or more norms in
order to permit their harmonious observance in effective pursuit of
the activity's purpose. If one is articulate, one can produce reasons
for one's solutions, one can make cases for them; the solutions are
not arbitrary. It sometimes happens, however, that it is difficult to
understand the character and purpose of the relevant activity and
the roles and points of the various norms that pertain to the activity.
There are disputes about the character of important activities and
domains. The field of jurisprudence, with its competing accounts of
what the law is and what it is for, offers complex examples of such
controversy. Similar disputes are found in many areas. Do problems
of resolving disputes about the point of a norm within an activity
and about the character of the activity itself reintroduce problems of
irreconcilable controversy and arbitrariness at a higher level? How
do we determine the nature of a practice? .

Consider again Dworkin's example of the rule prohibiting players
from unreasonably annoying one another during a chess match.
Dworkin suggests that the question of the relevance of this rule to
Tal's smiling is to be decided by reflecting on the character of the
game of chess. The point of the rule is to protect and foster in a certain way a game of a certain character, so we become clearer about
the point of the rule by making explicit the character of chess. How,
though, do we determine what the character of the game is? We turn
to actual practice; we consider how the game is played—what else is

3. The translation is by Philip Vellacott in *Euripides: Medea and Other Plays* (London: Penguin Books, 1963), pp. 117–18.

there to consider? Suppose, though, the character of the game is a matter of dispute; some players think chess is a contest involving, among other things, the ability to intimidate psychologically and the ability to resist such intimidation, while others believe that this is foreign to the nature of chess, that chess should be a contest that is decided by skills that are more "purely intellectual." Suppose further that this difference in belief is reflected in the play of these individuals. In this case, it appears that the character of chess as revealed in the way that the game is played would be indeterminate in just the respect in which it would need to be determinate to enable us to resolve the question of whether Tal's conduct is unreasonably annoying. Practice in certain areas reflects differences in beliefs about the character of activities. Such disagreements threaten to undermine the possibility of rational resolution of disagreements about the application of certain practical considerations by appeal to the point of the considerations. This is a very unsettling consequence, but it does accord with what sometimes happens when people disagree sharply about the character of an activity in which they engage. If there is sufficiently extensive disagreement about the character of our activities and the points of the considerations that pertain to them, then it is very likely that we will be unable to agree on solutions of difficult practical problems, including moral ones.

If we were to disagree extensively about the purposes of enough of our practices, then it would be very difficult for us to reach agreement by rational means about how to proceed. It is equally true, though, that it is often possible for members of a community to argue constructively with one another about the points of practical considerations and the purposes of their practices. Community presupposes a certain degree of agreement among its members about practices and purposes; community consists in people's living together, sharing practices and goals. It is by no means clear how much agreement is enough or what sort of agreement is needed. Phenomena such as the Protestant Reformation and the slavery issue in the United States in the nineteenth century are relevant but dauntingly complex. (Slavery is discussed below in Section 6 of this chapter.)

Dworkin's chess example is again helpful, this time in seeing how a case can be made for a certain conception of the character of a practice even though disagreements about its character are reflected in individuals' practice. Let us suppose that recently there has been a whole lot of psychological intimidation going on in chess. Some players study their opponents, searching for clues about the sorts of subtle behavior during a match that is likely to disconcert or distract them. Some players are able to use this strategy to advantage against certain opponents. They defend their conduct on the grounds that the ability to concentrate under competitive circumstances has always been a prerequisite for being able to compete in certain sorts of matches, that not everything that annoys is annoying behavior, and that the game of chess is enriched by adding to the competition the dimension of psychological conflict. Even though some players are actually playing in this way, believing that their conduct is appropriate, it is still possible to argue that their ploys are inconsistent with the character of chess. The case might be made by reference to past matches that are widely regarded as epitomizing excellence of play. One might argue that had the players in these classic games resorted to psychological intimidation, the particular excellences that the play in these games exemplifies would not have had free reign. The intrusion of "mind-games" would have interfered with the exercise of the skills so well exemplified in these classic matches, and the quality of play would have been lower.

The proponents of psychological intimidation in chess may reply that the results of the addition of the psychological ploys are sufficiently interesting to compensate for the diminution of the role of more purely intellectual skills in chess play. The argument threatens to terminate in an irresolvable difference of interests, but it need not do so. The chess purists here may argue that activities that exhibit skill at such intimidation do not cohere well with the exhibiting of traditional chess skills, that the countenancing of intimidation interferes with the exercise of these other skills. Of course, this claim would have to be supported by discussion of the various skills referred to here. Assuming that this claim could be supported, the argument, then, is that the introduction of intimidation into chess is the introduction of a discordant element into an existing game. It might be argued that certain of these intellectual skills have an interest and importance that goes beyond the playing of chess, that no other game gives these skills such prominence, while psychological intimidation is cultivated in many other games. A part of this argument, then, is what might be called an appreciation of the particular intellectual skills that are exercised in chess—an account of the importance of such skills in human life generally. Since chess without intimidation is a uniquely effective vehicle for the cultivation and exercise of important intellectual skills, the argument continues, the game with this character is worth preserving. Thus, steps to minimize the role of intimidation in chess are indicated.

This argument might not convince everyone. Perhaps some individuals simply fail to appreciate the value of intellectual skills. Others, while recognizing the superior value of these skills, might so enjoy chess with intimidation that they continue to play what they admit is a debased form of chess. It may be, though, that a case can be made for the importance of the skills required to play chess using psychological intimidation. It is conceivable that the chess community might divide on this issue so that there develop two importantly different forms of chess. Such a development might or might not be good for chess. That is, sometime in the future it might be possible to survey the development of the divided practice and make a case for the judgment that it has developed in interesting ways, that it continues to attract people of outstanding intellectual capacities, and so on. Or, on the other hand, it might be apparent that one or both of the games have gone into a decline.

4

The character of the game of chess is what reasonable people appeal to in making the case for the applicability of a rule in a hard case. Where the character of the game itself is in dispute, then the parties make claims about what chess is at its best or what is best in chess and ought to be preserved. In the end, though, people will decide how they want the game to be, and this will affect how they understand the rule about unreasonably annoying opponents. Whether Tal is in violation of the rule in smiling at Fischer rests, in the end, on what people decide chess is to be like.

It may seem that the proper solution of a serious problem about the applicability of a *moral* norm cannot be like the foregoing dispute about the relevance of a chess rule. What is morally right and wrong cannot be determined so readily by the decisions of people about the character of certain activities that they cultivate. In the chess example, everything depends upon people's deciding whether or not to make chess less purely intellectual. Such a matter might be decided simply by collective taste. This, it seems, is all there is to it. Surely, more is at stake in questions of the application of a moral norm. To solve a hard moral problem, there must be more to appeal to ultimately than people's naked preferences.

Of course, chess is a game. The solution of a hard problem about how chess should be played will affect primarily those who play chess, whereas the solution of a moral problem will be likely to have wider consequences. Even so, some people devote their lives to chess. For them, the character of the game is a very serious matter; they have much at stake in decisions about the character of the game. For their sakes, we would hope that the character of the game would not be decided in an offhand manner. The governing preferences here, moreover, are formed by a series of experiences with the actual playing of the game. How people want the game to be is determined very considerably by the game of chess itself. Their preferences about how the game should be are hardly "naked" preferences.

Sometimes there can be disagreement about the character of an activity, where the parties to the dispute can be said to represent two or more possible variants of the same activity. The imagined dispute about the character of chess illustrates this possibility. Sometimes, however, people make claims about the character of an activity that do not describe a possible variant of that activity; such characterizations are simply mistaken. Claims about the relevance of certain norms are sometimes based upon mistaken characterizations of the relevant activities; sometimes to resist such claims, it is enough to expose the mistake about the character of the activity.

As an example of a controversy about the relevance of certain moral considerations to an area of activity, where the argument turns upon mistaken claims about the character of the activity, consider the following. In a much discussed 1968 article in the *Harvard Business Review,* Albert Z. Carr maintained that business has its own ethics, different from ethics in other areas of life.[4] Business, Carr argues, is primarily a competition; entrepreneurs try to protect and advance their own positions at the expense of their competitors. The ethical precepts that apply to such noncompetitive spheres as family life and friendly cooperative undertakings—the Golden Rule, for example—do not apply to the activities of business. "A good part of the time the businessman is trying to do unto others as he hopes others will *not* do unto him"(146). It is wrong to deceive family members and friends in order to profit at their expense. Just as the form of deception known as bluffing in poker is an appropriate strategy in the competitive context of the poker game, so certain forms of competitive practice involving deception are appropriate in business—exaggerated claims in advertising (144), the marketing of shoddy products (144), and industrial espionage (145), for example. Carr does not maintain that anything goes in business. The practice of business, however, has its own standards, and these reflect the competitive character of the activity. The rules that serve as the ethics of business, according to Carr, are supplied by the positive law, by the explicit legislation that regulates the activity of business (148, 149).

Carr does not explain why he thinks that the ethics of business consists in the applicable portions of the positive law. Perhaps he thinks that an objective scrutiny of the activities of business reveals that the only ethical norms recognized by participants are provided by the law. In fact, in other words, business people compete within a framework of rules provided by the law; the law structures and defines their activities, just as the playing of a game is structured and defined by its rules. The law is sometimes broken in business, but the participants show by their reactions that they regard their illegal activity as cheating, whereas certain (legal) deceptive practices are accepted as fair. Actual practice shows that the ethics that pertains to other areas of life does not necessarily apply to business. This, in other words, is how the game is played.

This last position invites the criticism that it entails a form of unacceptable conventionalism; the view makes whatever people do

4. Albert Z. Carr, "Is Business Bluffing Ethical?" *Harvard Business Review* 46.1 (1968), 143–53. Page numbers in the text that follows refer to pages of this article. I am indebted to Roger Sullivan for bringing Carr's article to my attention.

the ultimate test of what is right, whereas actual practice is in fact sometimes morally objectionable.[5] One must, then, the objection continues, appeal to something other than actual practice in order to determine what standards of right and wrong apply to it. Suppose, though, Carr were to respond as follows: We are discussing a certain existing practice—business. It is a complex practice, but it is clearly a form of competition. Given what a competition is, it would be absurd for the participants to observe certain ethical norms that pertain to activities that are not competitive in character, standards that would not be coherent with the competitive character of business. This argument points to the appropriateness of certain norms, given the character of business activities, and to the inappropriateness of others. To argue in this way is not to foreclose the possibility of criticizing the existence of such a social practice as business competition. One might argue that the practice fails to do what it is supposed to do or that it interferes with other important activities and interests to such an extent that it is a liability. Whether one would be correct in such judgments would depend upon the actual practice of business and its effects on other practices that constitute the larger social context.

Carr's account is seriously mistaken, but the mistake is not in looking in the nature of the activity itself for norms applicable to the practice. Rather, Carr goes wrong in the account he offers of the nature of business activity. He misdescribes the practice—his account of it is narrow and incomplete. When a more accurate account is given of actual practice and its purposes, it becomes apparent that some of the ethical norms that Carr claims—implausibly—are irrelevant to business are indeed applicable. Business activities, as Carr says, have a competitive aspect, but they are not *just* competitions with winners and losers. Business activities provide goods and services to clients and customers; activities that were not directed at fulfilling such a function would not be *business* activities. Relevant to the performance of certain business activities—those directed at the needs and interests of clients—are standards of excellence appropri-

5. See, for example, Norman Chase Gillespie, "The Business of Ethics," in *Profits and Professions: Essays in Business and Professional Ethics,* ed. Wade L. Robinson, Michael S. Pritchard, and Joseph S. Ellin (Clifton, N.J.: Humana Press, 1983), pp. 133–40.

ate to the character of the service provided. Such standards have to do with the performance of the service up to a certain level of competence. One who provides shoddy goods and services does badly as a provider. Customers and clients—those to whom the provider has undertaken to provide the services or goods—have grounds for complaining that the provision is unsatisfactory. Their complaints are not answered by pointing out that the provider prevailed in competition with rival providers, making a profit on the transaction and ensuring that competitors did not profit from it. The relationship of providers to customers is, in a broad sense, a contractual one; their dealings with one another have characteristics of cooperative activities. They have responsibilities, obligations to one another that derive from these dealings. A customer may be cheated by shoddy provision, whether or not the law is violated. Builders, perhaps, are engaged in beating out the competition, but this is not *all* they are doing (and this is not what makes them builders). Their activity by its very nature is aimed at serving people's interests in specific ways. Relevant to their activity are norms of evaluation that reflect the concern with how well these interests are served. This is undeniably part of the practice of business, too.

My criticism of Carr's argument is inspired by Plato's *Republic*. In Book I, the character Socrates attacks the claim of Thrasymachus that the best rulers of a *polis* are those who single-mindedly seek their own advantage at the expense of those whom they rule. Socrates argues that the activity of ruling, like navigating and healing, is one that provides a certain service for clients. How well an individual does at such activities is determined to a large extent by how well clients are served in the relevant way. Ruling is an activity whose central purpose is to protect and foster in certain ways the welfare of the ruled. Thrasymachus's conception of the nature of ruling is grossly mistaken, and so, as a result, is his account of the norms by which ruling is judged to be done well or badly.[6]

One of the central themes of Plato's luminous *Republic*—the idea that a community is a group of people organized by a coordinated division of labor—is relevant to the determination of the character of certain important activities. The activities of people engaged in busi-

6. Compare Plato, *The Republic*, Book 1, 341 c–342 e.

ness are part of a social system involving an elaborate scheme of division of labor. Business practices affect the economic welfare of entire communities, and citizens who are neither clients nor competitors may criticize particular business practices by appeal to certain norms of citizenship. In the course of their characteristic activities, business people encounter others as clients, customers, employees, fellow citizens—they do not deal only with competitors. The characters of these various relationships reflect the activities in which the participants are engaged. In a free-market economy, business activity involves competition with other business people, provision of goods and services to customers and clients, fulfilling a role in the economy of a community, and public activity of a member taking part in the life of a polity. The norms that pertain to all of these activities are relevant to the practice of business—because of the character of business activities, because of the nature of these and other activities.

In the social context in which Carr was writing, the complexity of actual business activities, the variety of purposes, and the multiplicity of standards of assessment that can be relevant make certain sorts of conflicts of considerations inevitable in business. An entrepreneur has obligations to investors and employees to be competitive, to protect investments, and to make a profit. It may be difficult to compete successfully and at the same time to provide clients with goods and service of acceptable quality. These two considerations sometimes reinforce one another, but sometimes they conflict. Actual business activity tends to strike a compromise between these matters, often an uneasy compromise.

This sort of conflict, inevitable in the existing social circumstances, should be faced squarely and dealt with intelligently—with an attention to all relevant concerns. Carr's view of business blinds him to a wide range of considerations that are relevant to its practice. Not only does Carr misrepresent the actual character of business activities, but, in conceiving of business as simply a game-like competition, he envisions it as a compartmentalized activity substantially insulated from the wider social context, the larger life of the community in which it takes place. His practical judgments and decisions, as a result, can be expected to be unsatisfactory. The remedy is a more accurate and comprehensive description of the activities, purposes, and norms involved in business and the actual relationships of business to the larger social context. The relevance of a wide range of moral considerations is then apparent.

Disagreements about the character and purpose of a certain activity, then, even those differences that are reflected in actual practice, can be adjudicated by considering the coherence of the practice under competing conceptions and the importance of the matters given prominence by the competing conceptions. Sometimes we find that we have simply misdescribed familiar practices, even very familiar ones in which we are frequent participants. In these cases, it is often sufficient to have the mistake brought to our attention in order to see that it is a mistake. Carr's account of the nature of business activities involves such a mistake. In his preoccupation with the competitive aspects of business, he loses sight of features of such activities that are so central to them that we cannot imagine what the activities would be like without the features. Thrasymachus makes a similar mistake about the nature of ruling.

In other disputes, however, we are confronted with two or more clearly articulated variants of a practice, and the disagreement concerns which variant to adopt. The possibility of success in resolving disputes of this latter sort among reasonable people depends upon discovering the properly situated areas of agreement among the parties. There is no guarantee that this is possible, but if the parties are members of the same community, there will necessarily be extensive areas of agreement among them about a variety of practices and purposes. This point would lead us to expect that disagreements among individuals who are not members of the same community will be more difficult to resolve, and this is in fact what we find.

5

When there is disagreement about the nature and purpose of a practice, it is not always clear whether the disagreement is due to one or more misunderstandings of the activity or whether there are two or more different conceptions of the activity, each more or less viable. When the disputes concern complex institutions and practices, such as law, government, education, or commerce, it may be very difficult to sort these things out. Chess, after all, is only a game, and so it is an example of a particularly compact and compartmentalized social practice. Similar points might be made, however, about disagreements concerning larger, more momentous practices that interpenetrate one another. The dispute about whether "creation science" should be taught in public schools as an alternative to evolutionary biology requires us to consider, among other things, the character of scientific inquiry, and the issue has interesting parallels to Dworkin's chess example.[7]

The actual practice of judges in deciding hard cases is influenced by their conception of the law as a complex human activity. Where conceptions differ, we would expect disagreement among judges about certain cases, and this is what we find. We should expect too that competing conceptions of the law in jurisprudence sometimes offer viable alternative variants of the activities that comprise the law and sometimes represent misunderstandings of this domain.

In *Law's Empire* (*LE*), Ronald Dworkin argues that judges should try in deciding hard cases "to find, in some coherent set of principles about people's rights and duties, the best constructive interpretation of the political structure and legal doctrine of their community. They try to make that complex structure and record the best these can be."[8] His discussion of the nineteenth-century case of *Riggs v. Palmer* may serve as a partial illustration of this very complex conception (*LE* 15–20). This case concerned a man murdered by his grandson who was also his heir. After being convicted of the crime, the grandson claimed the portion of his victim's estate that was left to him in the grandfather's will. The other members of the family contested this claim. New York statutes at the time said nothing explicitly barring a legatee from inheriting after murdering the testator. There were no obviously applicable legal precedents. When the case reached the highest court of appeal in New York State, one member of the court argued that the murderer should inherit, since the testator had clearly indicated that was his wish in a valid will. Testators should be able to

---

7. See the January 5, 1982, decision in *McClean v. Arkansas* by Judge William R. Overton, reprinted in *Science*, February 19, 1982, 934–43. Judge Overton argues, among other things, that what is called "creation science" is not science.

8. Ronald Dworkin, *Law's Empire* (Cambridge: Harvard University Press, 1986), p. 255.

be confident that if they draw up a will properly, their wishes will be respected. This opinion, however, did not prevail. A majority of the court found that the murderer was not entitled to inherit, on the grounds that it is not the intent of the statutes that govern wills that the murderer of the testator should be able to inherit under the will in this way, thus profiting from his crime. It is a deeply embedded principle of the law that the law should not allow itself to be used by criminals so that they can profit by their crimes. In the absence of evidence to the contrary, it is reasonable to suppose that the legislators who made the law on wills would have rejected the idea, had they thought of it, that such a murderer could use the law to profit from his crime. So, a majority of the judges on the highest court of appeal in New York State found that the grandson was not entitled to inherit.

Wills are legal instruments that enable individuals to make certain of their wishes effective after their death. The law of wills, then, performs this function. The minority opinion in *Riggs v. Palmer* based its argument on this point. The majority opinion is based upon the understanding that the law has many purposes, including opposing injustices such as murder. To permit a murderer to use the law of wills to profit from his crime is to allow the law to be co-opted into complicity with criminal injustice. The law is more coherent if the principle that criminals should not profit from their wrongs that holds elsewhere in the law is understood to hold too in the law of wills (*LE* 19–20).

The reasoning of the majority in this case is consistent with Dworkin's general account of how judges should reason. Is there a viable alternative conception of judicial decision implicit in the minority reasoning in *Riggs v. Palmer*? Dworkin understands this alternative as the position that judges should consider the meaning of statutes and legal principles in isolation from one another. In other words, judges should understand and apply the law of wills independently of the rest of the law. We should strive to understand and apply statutes "literally," in an "acontextual" way.

We know from experience that we cannot formulate rules that will anticipate every contingency in a given activity, and we know too that if we attempt to apply single rules to conduct, without considering the point of what we are doing and what else is at stake, the result is apt to be unsatisfactory. If this piecemeal approach to the law were adopted generally, then a certain rigidity would prevail. We would be forced to accept results in unanticipated cases that no sensible person would want. The law would be a stupid thing.[9] Of course, we do not want judges to have the power to replace laws with their own ideas at their discretion—this would defeat much of the purpose of having such laws as norms in the first place. Judges are bound by the purposes of the various devices that the law creates, and they are bound by the many legal norms that already exist. Their task, properly, is to interpret these norms in particular cases, in an attempt to preserve the many purposes of the law and the harmony of legal norms as a whole. This is an application of the general point that reasonableness in following any norm is a matter of observing the norm in conjunction with other norms that pertain in the pursuit of one or more activities. Whether or not the conception of judicial deciding implicit in the minority decision is viable, its general implementation would be highly undesirable.

On the conception of the law implicit in the majority decision in *Riggs v. Palmer*, the law is a better social practice than it is on the minority conception. It is a better instrument for realizing the many important purposes it serves. Just as one should interpret a poem in such a way that it comes off as well as possible as the sort of poem it is, Dworkin argues, so one should interpret social practices so that they are understood as being "the best they can be."[10] My question was whether the law as conceived by the minority position in *Riggs* is viable. Perhaps it is marginally viable. It is possible to pursue a practice in ways that are less rather than more effective in serving

9. See H. L. A. Hart, *The Concept of Law* (Oxford: Clarendon Press, 1961), chap. 7, especially pp. 123–27.

10. When practitioners appeal to the character of an activity in deciding how to apply various norms, they do indeed search for an understanding of the practice according to which the practice comes off better rather than worse. The comparison of this sort of determination with interpreting a poem, however, has its limitations. In interpreting a poem, one is interpreting something that is literally a symbol, whereas social practices are not symbols in the same sense. Normally, too, the interpretation of a poem does not have the practical consequences, the influence on the conduct of a group of people, that judges' understanding of the law as a social institution has. This, I suspect, is connected with the individualism in Dworkin's account of interpretation of the law that Gerald J. Postema discusses in " 'Protestant' Interpretation and Social Practices," *Law and Philosophy* 6 (1987), 283–319. In the first chapter of his *Natural Law and Natural Rights* (Oxford: Clarendon Press, 1980), John Finnis provides a useful alternative account of understanding a social practice.

the purposes of the practice—that is, it is possible to proceed in ways that are less rather than more intelligent. If judges decide hard cases by attempting to understand the law in ways that serve all its many purposes, things will go better in the legal domain than if judges adopt a piecemeal approach.

6

Some modifications of practices extend the practices in new directions in ways that cohere with the aims and standards of the originals, in ways that constitute a development and enhancement of them. Such modifications would be so far consistent with the character of the practice, even though the modifications at the same time represent a significant change in the practice. Other modifications, however, may be more or less discordant with the original practice; these introduce into the practice elements that are at odds with the original character of the practice. When the chess purist claims that psychological intimidation is incompatible with the character of the game, the claim means that the innovation clashes with, interferes with, what chess at its very best has been. The complaint is that rather than extending and enhancing chess, the change makes the game less coherent, in a way that interferes with its valuable aspects.

An activity is a social artifact; when one talks about the character of the activity, one refers to what practitioners do. What practitioners do that is relevant to ascertaining the character of an activity such as chess, however, is not restricted merely to how they move pieces on a chess board and how they comport themselves between moves. Equally important are their evaluations of the play of themselves and others, their aspirations, purposes, and valuations in connection with the activity, and their understanding of how the activity affects other endeavors (the "larger life"). The character of the activity, then, will be given by its practice in accordance with all the standards that pertain to the activity. What standards properly pertain may be a matter of controversy, but there are intellectual resources for fruitful debate about such differences.

What, though, of activities and practices that effectively serve important needs and interests that are nonetheless evil practices? On the view that norms are internal to activities and get their character and authority from these activities, by what standard can the wickedness of such practices be determined? Slavery, for example, has existed at one time or another in most communities.[11] It has at times provided labor for important tasks, it has enriched considerable numbers of individuals, and perhaps it has on occasion raised the standard of living of communities. Insofar as realizing such results constitutes fulfilling the purpose of this practice, it can be judged a success on its own terms, by its own standards. On the view that norms are internal to practices, how are we to articulate and defend the conviction that slavery is an evil practice?

The simplest answer to this objection begins with the observation that practices do not occur in isolation from one another. Thus an important consideration in the assessment of any practice is its effect on other practices and upon the life of the community. Although a practice may serve important needs and interests, it is always relevant to ask, at what cost? In order to answer this question, it is necessary to consider the social setting in which the practice takes place and its effects on the other areas of life. Activities and practices, to a greater or lesser extent, interpenetrate one another. Slavery is not a social atom that merely happens from time to time to impact upon other social phenomena. Slavery could not be the *only* existing social practice. Slavery presupposes such things as cooperative activity, labor and services, ownership, authority—there could be no such thing as slavery apart from these and other social artifacts. People who take part in a practice such as slavery necessarily *at the same time* participate in other practices that have their own standards and norms. To engage in a practice that is a success on its own terms may be at the same time to violate the norms of other practices that one participates in at the same time.

So, for example, many slaveowners and slave traders in the United States in the mid-nineteenth century depended for their livelihood upon the practice. Their fortunes were invested in it and inseparable from it. They carried on their business, however, in a

11. According to Orlando Patterson, "There is no region on earth that has not at some time harbored the institution. Probably there is no group of people whose ancestors were not at one time slaves or slaveholders." See his *Slavery and Social Death: A Comparative Study* (Cambridge: Harvard University Press, 1982), p. vii.

community that was committed to democratic and egalitarian political ideals. These norms are deeply incompatible with the practice of slavery, and the social and political fabric of the country at this time was riven by the existence of slavery in it.

It will be objected that the important thing about slavery is that it is *inherently* evil; this sort of badness is not accounted for by pointing out that slavery happens to conflict with *other* things. To show the inherent wickedness of slavery, the objection continues, it is necessary to establish its badness independently of its effects on anything else. How, though, are we to determine the boundary between slavery and "other things"? Activities and practices current in a community are not separable from one another like pieces of a jigsaw puzzle. People who participate in a practice of slavery are ipso facto at the same time participating in other institutions and practices. They are at the same time engaging in agriculture or manufacture; they are taking part in the life of a political community that will have its own well-developed norms. Why should not the evaluation of slavery involve a consideration of its relationships with these other matters?

It will be objected that arguing that slavery is wrong by appeal to the norms of our particular egalitarian political morality fails to show that slavery is wrong in other communities where the political morality is quite different. It can be argued, I think, that slavery, by its very nature, is a bad practice in a wide variety of social and cultural situations. Slavery involves making certain individuals entirely subject to the wills of other people. Individuals in this situation are in a precarious position; the wills that govern their lives are not their own. Their masters are not likely to be as concerned about slaves' desires and welfare as the slaves themselves are. Slaves are vulnerable to the indifference, cruelty, and malice of others. In fact, we find that slaves are almost everywhere wretched and oppressed. The cruelties inherent in this situation, the hatred and resentment generated, lead to a deep division in a community. Continual coercion and the threat of violence are necessary in order to maintain such a practice. A community so divided is flawed and weakened. This argument, of course, is an attempt to show that the costs of slavery are apt to be excessive. It will not satisfy those who claim that even in a social situation where happy slaves lived harmoniously with kind and generous masters slavery would be a bad practice. We do not know, however, that such a thing is possible, nor do we have a clear enough idea of what such a social situation would be like to know whether or not slavery would be bad in such circumstances.[12]

An illustration that John Dewey used in discussing similar issues is helpful here.[13] In his satirical essay on the discovery of roast pig, Charles Lamb described the following serendipitous event: A pig wandered into a house and subsequently perished when the building burned. People sifting through the ruins accidentally touched the hot carcass of the pig, burned their fingers, and put their injured hands in their mouths to soothe them. They were so pleased with the taste they discovered, that they commenced to build buildings, imprison pigs inside, burn down the buildings, and feast in the ashes. One interesting feature of the procedure described is that it achieves its purpose; Lamb describes an effective way of producing roast pig. Nonetheless, the story is a joke; what these people do after their initial discovery is absurd. It is absurd because of the preposterous cost of the means of producing the tasty dish. We understand what is involved in building buildings and the importance that buildings have; destroying buildings for taste treats is unthinkable, especially when other ways of roasting pork are readily available. What would be the point here in saying that because Lamb's procedure for producing roast pork is an effective way of achieving this purpose, it is not *inherently* absurd? Part of the procedure described is that it involves building buildings and burning them down. Buildings and the resources needed to produce them have a certain value. Perhaps we can imagine social circumstances quite different from ours in which this procedure would not be absurd, but such circumstances have no relevance to our own. Similarly, slavery involves making the wills of some people entirely subordinate to the wills of others. We know the value of what is lost in this subjugation, and we know the effects of this loss on the relationships of people to one another as they attempt to live together and pursue together

12. See Michael Walzer, *Spheres of Justice* (New York: Basic Books, 1983), p. 250n.
13. John Dewey, *Theory of Valuation* (1939) in *John Dewey: The Later Works, 1925–1953*, vol. 13, ed. Jo Ann Boydston (Carbondale: Southern Illinois University Press, 1991), pp. 226–30. Frederick Will brought this example to my attention.

the activities that are implicated in slavery. Perhaps we can imagine social circumstances very different from our own in which the value of what is lost in slavery is not exorbitant, but this will not justify establishing slavery in any actual circumstance we know of.

7

My aim is to exploit certain neglected similarities between the sort of practical knowledge involved in morality and the practical knowledge necessary to pursue such activities as building, commerce, inquiring, governing, and so on. Morality, on this view, is practical knowledge consisting of a variety of different items that apply to a wide range of activities. The items of knowledge themselves that make up this conglomerate are the results of a community's experience over a long time with a variety of different problems. Morality, on this view, is like other practical knowledge in that it is changeable, improvable. In the course of using such knowledge, people necessarily change it; sometimes they improve it. Good cognitive practice in dealing with moral problems is analogous to good problem-solving in any activity. Certain other views in moral philosophy promise that if one gets the theory right—that is, if one gives an accurate account of good cognitive practice in moral matters—then the resolution of practical problems will be made easy. Solutions will simply fall out of the theory. Insofar as morality is like other bodies of practical knowledge, however, all moral problems will not be solved in this way in the abstract. The more interesting ones will require applying practical knowledge to a very particular set of circumstances that present unprecedented difficulties. Theory can help in this most difficult intellectual task: it is always useful to have a clear conception of the task at hand and an appreciation of what is involved. To resolve the concrete problems, however, one must be a practitioner.

5. Practical Knowledge and Will

Morality is described in the preceding chapters as a collection of items of practical knowledge characterized by their importance and their general applicability across many practical domains. The view that morality consists of practical *knowledge* will strike some as an excessively intellectualized conception of ethics. Morality is more than knowledge and understanding, it will be urged—it has to do with affect, motivation, the will. We are all too familiar with selfish, callous, greedy individuals, who know perfectly well what morality requires of them in their behavior toward others, who nonetheless persist in villainy. Some of these people are wretched, conflicted souls, tormented by shame and remorse; others, however, are relatively unperturbed by the knowledge of their own wickedness. Knowing what one should do according to certain standards is not always sufficient for doing it. Being a good person is not just a matter of knowing what one should do; it requires in addition a certain condition of the will, a determination to follow the norms of morality. Morality, then, is not (just) a matter of practical knowledge.

But consider: Medicine is a body of practical knowledge, if anything is. Yet there are physicians who have mastered this body of practical knowledge—competent physicians who know as well as anyone how to treat various medical conditions—who do not practice well as physicians. They know what they are required to do by the standards of their art, but they engage in what they recognize as shoddy medical practice. So, for example, certain surgeons perform surgery that is not in their patients' best interests, in order to make money or to perfect surgical skills or to fulfill institutional quotas. Being a good physician—one who practices medicine well—consists in more than just the possession of medical knowledge. So much seems clearly true. Does it follow, then, that medicine is not a body of practical knowledge?

The view that morality is a collection of items of practical knowledge, whose origin and authority is similar to medicine, appears to be at odds with David Hume's influential doctrine that morals are "not derived from reason alone." Here is Hume's most impressive argument for this thesis:

> Since morals . . . have an influence on the actions and affections, it follows, that they cannot be deriv'd from reason; and that because reason alone, as we have already prov'd, can never have any such influence. Morals excite passions, and produce or prevent actions. Reason of itself is utterly impotent in this particular. The rules of morality, therefore, are not conclusions of our reason.[1]

Hume's argument might be reconstructed in the following way: Morality is essentially a practical matter; that is, moral standards and the judgments based upon these standards are meant to influence, to guide conduct. But the mere knowledge that something is the case does not necessarily influence anyone's actions. In order for knowledge to influence individuals' actions, it must touch upon some concern that they have, some matter that they desire to secure or avoid.[2] No judgment, therefore, no matter how validly inferred from other truths, will qualify as a moral judgment unless it touches upon some general concern—unless, in Hume's terminology, it evokes some "sentiment." Hume concluded, "It is impossible that the distinction betwixt moral good and evil can be made by reason; since that distinction has an influence upon our actions, of which reason alone is incapable" (*Treatise*, 3.1.1, p. 462). "Morality, therefore, is more properly felt than judged of" (*Treatise*, 3.1.2, p. 470).

1. David Hume, *A Treatise of Human Nature*, ed. L. A. Selby-Bigge, 2d ed. revised by P. H. Nidditch (Oxford: Clarendon Press, 1978), book 3, part 1, Section 1, p. 457.
2. Cf. Hume, *Treatise*, 2.3.3, especially pp. 413–15.

This particular argument entitles Hume to conclude that in order to account for the distinctly *practical* character of morality, we must note that it is built upon certain very widely shared concerns—matters that engage the desires, hopes, and fears of people generally. This follows immediately from the action-guiding function of morality and from the relevance of this guide to people in all areas of life. It does not follow, of course, that every moral judgment directly engages the concerns of every person. If we attend to what the argument actually establishes about the role of affect in moral knowledge, it is apparent that a similar conclusion can be established for *any* body of practical knowledge. That is, to account for its practical character, its action-guiding function, we must note that the knowledge has to do with the securing or avoidance of things that at least some people are generally concerned to secure or avoid. This does not imply, however, that every knowledgeable individual on every occasion will be sufficiently motivated to secure the very things the practical knowledge is designed to secure. On too many occasions, the absence of sufficient motivation or the presence of strong conflicting concerns in an individual may result in practice that is discrepant with respect to the standards implicit in the relevant body of practical knowledge. Still, though, if the knowledge is practical, then, to the extent that the knowledge is effective, practice exists that answers to specific concerns that people have—there exist things that people really care about that the knowledge aids them in addressing. This holds for practical knowledge generally, including morality.

2

The claim that morality is a collection of items of practical knowledge needs to be distinguished from the claim that virtue—good character—consists in nothing more than knowledge. The Socratic thesis that such traits of character as justice, courage, and temperance consist simply in knowledge of what one should do in certain circumstances is open to well-known objections.[3] Being a good person

3. See Terence Irwin, *Plato's Moral Theory* (Oxford: Clarendon Press, 1977), pp. 75–77.

consists in more than knowing what one should do, just as being a good practitioner of the healing art consists in more than knowing how to heal.

Plato claimed:

> The rest of the world are of the opinion . . . that a man may have knowledge, and yet that the knowledge which is in him may be overmastered by anger, or pleasure, or pain, or love, or perhaps by fear—just as if knowledge were nothing but a slave and might be dragged about by all these other things. . . . Knowledge [however] is a noble thing and fit to command in man, which cannot be overcome and will not allow a man, if he only knows the good and the evil, to do anything which is contrary to what his knowledge bids him do.[4]

There are counterexamples to Plato's claim that knowledge cannot be "overcome" that exemplify such phenomena as *akrasia* and self-deception, but people also choose quite deliberately to act contrary to certain norms, to certain items of practical knowledge. The mastery of a body of practical knowledge of any sort is not sufficient for straining to do well by its standards on every occasion. The norms of practical knowledge will not automatically overwhelm every other concern. Lewis Carroll's Achilles, frustrated by the Tortoise's persistent refusal to draw the conclusion indicated by the rules of inference, warns the Tortoise that logic will lay hands on him. Our recognition of the futility of this threat is based upon our knowing that such norms and standards do not influence us by *force majeur*. However important the rules of inference may be, their "force" is more like the force of custom than the force of arms, and the Tortoise was more interested in being philosophically provocative (and perhaps irritating as well).[5] This point, despite Plato, holds for other norms besides logical ones.

4. Plato, *Protagoras*, 352 b-c. The translation is that of B. Jowett, revised by Martin Ostwald, in *Plato's Protagoras*, ed. Gregory Vlastos (New York: Liberal Arts Press, 1956).

5. ' "Now that you accept A and B and C and D, *of course* you accept Z."

"Do I?" said the Tortoise innocently. "Let's make that quite clear. I accept A, B, C, and D. Suppose I *still* refuse to accept Z?"

"Then logic would take you by the throat, and *force* you to do it!" Achilles triumphantly replied.'

Lewis Carroll, "What the Tortoise Said to Achilles," *Mind*, n.s. 4, no. 14 (April 1895), 278–80.

3

Although the possession of practical knowledge is not itself logically sufficient for striving to act in accordance with its standards on every occasion, *what* one possesses is something focused on and structured by specific matters of general concern. A particular body of practical knowledge, its norms, and the interests and concerns it serves are thoroughly and complexly interconnected, interwoven. The particular concerns the knowledge serves are its raison d'être; they are also major determinants in shaping the knowledge as it develops. These concerns and the body of knowledge mold one another; each reflects the other. In the pursuit of a certain practice, the discovery of new possibilities frequently affects the aims and interests of practitioners. Individuals who master a complex practice acquire an understanding of how certain results are produced, but they typically develop new interests. They come to appreciate, moreover, the importance of many factors that they learn to recognize as helps or hindrances in their pursuits. The process of learning involves both affect and cognition in reciprocal interaction with one another; it is as much a matter of the development of new interests and concerns as it is a matter of acquiring information. A complex set of concerns is thereby produced, and some of these concerns are fully comprehensible only in the context of the practice. Such concerns are "internal" to one or more practices.[6] Elegance in mathematical proofs, profit maximization in business, explanatory power in scientific theorizing, and control of an opponent in amateur wrestling are examples of common concerns of practitioners that require for their comprehension the understanding of a practice.

"Reason is, and ought only to be the slave of the passions, and can never pretend to any other office than to serve and obey them," David Hume proclaimed.[7] The practical knowledge that belongs to a practice, however, is not necessarily subordinate to the concerns the practice serves in the way Hume's master-slave metaphor would suggest. Here, "reason" and "passion" are apt to be more like long-time partners who have influenced one another in the course of their associa-

6. Alasdair MacIntyre develops the idea of goods internal to a practice. See his *After Virtue*, pp. 187–91.

7. Hume, *Treatise*, 2.3.3, p. 415.

tion. How they and their joint enterprise came to be as they are can be understood only in the history of their cooperative interaction. They are functioning, interacting, evolving elements in an organic whole.

To characterize morality, then, as a collection of items of practical knowledge is not to deny that human desires and passions are centrally involved in it. Indeed, this view strongly suggests that there are human concerns that are internal to morality and that the interests that morality serves are important determinants of its form, its nature. In looking at the characters of good people, we are looking at the interests, concerns, appreciations, and know-how required to act well in a wide variety of human activities. We are examining the ways in which an individual person is shaped by engaging in shared activities in accordance with the purposes and norms proper to those activities. It is well said that virtues play functional roles in a common life.[8] Virtues are whatever combination or combinations of interests, concerns, appreciations, habits, and know-how consistently result in acting well in various ways in a variety of shared activities. When we study virtues, then, we are not studying something distinct from actions and the norms that pertain to them. The virtues are best conceived in Aristotelian terms as dispositions whose full actuality consists in pursuing activities in accordance with the many pertinent norms. Good character is whatever concatenation of psychological dispositions reliably realizes itself in acting well. The focus in the study of virtues must be on the good actions that are their full actualization. "Virtue ethics," then, should not be conceived as an alternative to the study of norms and activities.

4

If we take seriously the idea that morality is a collection of items of practical knowledge, in important ways similar to medicine or navigation, it is immediately apparent how to offer a naturalistic account of ethics and how to account for its authority and importance.

8. Edmund L. Pincoffs, *Quandaries and Virtues: Against Reductivism in Ethics* (Lawrence: University Press of Kansas, 1986), pp. 6ff. See also James D. Wallace, *Virtues and Vices* (Ithaca: Cornell University Press, 1978), chap. 1.

The existence of morality is to be understood historically; it is a social artifact, like the positive law or metallurgy. Its authority is to be understood in terms of the importance of the interests it serves and the effectiveness in promoting those interests of the know-how it represents.

This is a line of thought that clearly tempted Plato and Aristotle; they took seriously such a view, though their positions concerning it are complex. Plato accepted the Socratic position that virtue is knowledge, although he rejected the identification of virtue with craft-knowledge. One decisive point for Plato appears to be that one cannot identify the *product* of an excellence of character as one can identify the product of a *techne*. The skilled potter knows how to make pots; what does the *dikaios* (the "just" or righteous individual) know how to make? The absence of a material product is not the issue; navigators know how to find their way safely at sea; what do the *dikaioi* know how to do? More generally, one goes to a physician for medicine, a navigator for a travel-plan; what does one go to the *dikaios* for?[9]

Consider this answer to Plato's question: The honest person knows how to follow a certain norm in a number of different practical domains. This individual knows how to follow a norm of non-deception in concert with other pertinent norms in several activities. The *techne* of the navigator, the farmer, the physician is a mastery of a single specific activity; the know-how of the *dikaios* pertains to a single norm that recurs in many activities. This provides a response to the criticism implicit in the Platonic question, "One goes to a potter for pots, a navigator to find one's course—what does one go to a *dikaios* for?"

The claim that *dikaiosune* is simply knowing how to follow a certain norm in concert with other norms in several unspecified practical domains is open to another of Plato's (and Aristotle's) objections to the claim that an excellence of character is a species of craft-knowledge, a *techne*. The objection is that a specific sort of know-how can be used intentionally to produce the very opposite of its defining purpose: so a physician's knowledge can be used to produce suffering and death; navigational knowledge can be used to guide a ship onto a reef and sink it. Know-how can be exhibited in effectively producing its defining purpose and also the opposite

9. *Republic*, 332c–333e.

of this purpose. Know-how is not sufficient for right action in the sphere of medicine or navigation. An excellence of character, however, consists in more than know-how; it also involves the concern that the knowledge of how to follow the norm be used properly.[10]

This point of Plato's is right, but it does not foreclose the possibility that the norm with which an honest person is concerned is itself an item of practical knowledge—something one would have to know how to observe properly to qualify as an honest person. The existence of this norm N as one of a number of norms to be observed simultaneously in the proper performance of activity A is to be attributed to the understanding that the proper observance of N contributes to the practice of A, to the realization of A's purpose. N in activity B will contribute to B's practice and the realization of its purpose, and so on. The existence and authority of N is no different in principle from the existence and authority of any of the norms that pertain to A or B.

Aristotle denied that virtues of character (*aretai ethikai*) are arts or crafts (*technai*), on the grounds that the latter are directed at making (*poiesis*) while the former are concerned with doing (*praxis*).[11] The know-how of the potter is directed at bringing pots into being, whereas the virtue truthfulness is exhibited in acts that are not necessarily directed at producing anything. The art, the know-how, of a particular individual, moreover, is not itself an excellence; one can have the requisite knowledge of building yet not build well, not be a good practitioner of the art. A virtue such as truthfulness, on the other hand, is itself an excellence; one has it in virtue of possessing the tendency, the dynamic disposition to act *well* in a certain respect: "*Phronesis* (practical wisdom), then, must be a reasoned and true state of capacity to act with regard to human goods. . . . While there is such a thing as excellence in *techne* (art), there is no such thing as excellence in *phronesis* ; and in *techne* he who errs willingly is preferable, but in *phronesis*, as in the virtues, he is the reverse. Plainly, then, *phronesis* is a virtue and not a *techne*."[12]

10. *Republic*, 333e–334b.
11. *Nicomachean Ethics*, 1140a 3–24. In this discussion, I ignore the technical senses Aristotle gave to *praxis* and *poiesis*.
12. *Nicomachean Ethics*, 1140b 20–25. The translation is that of W. D. Ross in *The Works of Aristotle Translated into English*, vol. 9, ed. W. D. Ross (Oxford: Clarendon Press, 1915). I have replaced certain English words with Greek.

Practical knowledge or art in a person is not the same thing as an excellence, a tendency to do well. So far Aristotle is right. The claim that morality consists in a collection of items of practical knowledge, however, does not entail the mistaken claim that excellences of character—courage, honesty, compassion—are themselves simply items of practical knowledge. Morality is not itself a virtue or a set of virtues, any more than it is a desire or a set of desires; morality, in the sense of a set of valued ways of acting, however, has its counterpart in the aspirations and dispositions of its adherents. In the end, any practical knowledge will exist in the activity of those individuals who possess it, and their activity will be explained in terms of their knowledge and the interests, the concerns of theirs, that the knowledge serves.

Aristotle is also right in claiming that a virtue such as truthfulness is not necessarily exhibited in the production of some particular kind of thing in the way that the know-how of a potter is. It is not true, however, that the activities that exhibit truthfulness are necessarily distinct from productive activities or that its status as an excellence is independent of the purposes we have in productive and other activities. Truthfulness is a virtue that is exhibited in a variety of activities, including productive activities. It is a virtue of (moral) character because it promotes important human purposes in a wide variety of undertakings. It is a tendency to act well in accordance with certain norms that pertain widely across a broad range of human activities, but those norms themselves are important in those various activities because they tend to promote the purposes that people have in engaging in these and other particular activities.

5

Consider, for example, the role of truthfulness in scientific research. It is obviously crucial to the practice of inquiry that scientists describe their work accurately to themselves and their colleagues. No one who cares about science can be indifferent to this consideration; the realization of the central purpose(s) of scientific research depends in obvious ways upon scrupulous attention to truth and accuracy in communication among scientists. The possession of a cultivated concern for the dissemination of accurate information among scientists is a virtue of scientists. The standards of excellence that pertain to scientific work reflect the importance of accuracy and truthfulness in the enterprise. Anyone who cares about science and the standards of excellence that pertain to it will have reason to value truthfulness in scientists. One can, perhaps, imagine scenarios in which someone who cares nothing at all about science nevertheless goes through the arduous training necessary to be a researcher. If such a person remains indifferent to the concerns that are internal to science, even after having taken part in scientific research, it is difficult to see what can be done to imbue the individual with these concerns. Such scientific researchers, however, will be exceptional, abnormal. Generally those who take the trouble to master the art of scientific research will care about science and its concerns; it will be the interests and concerns of these scientists that guide the development of the practice. The possession of the practical knowledge—the know-how—requisite for research will be accompanied by a concern for the cultivation of scientific knowledge in accordance with the appropriate standards and an appreciation of the importance of truthfulness in its pursuit. The *understanding* of the importance of truthfulness in research will be, in a person who cares about research, an *appreciation* of its value in research. Practical knowledge normally involves appreciating the importance of certain things, valuing things. People engaged in scientific research know the importance of truthfulness and are so far motivated to be truthful with one another. This can be taken as a description of the way in which both "reason" and "sentiment" are internally related in an actual practical domain. Both the similarities and the differences between this description and Hume's general account of this matter are important.

It will sometimes happen that a researcher is in a position that demands immediate results of a certain degree of scientific significance—for example, a case needs to be made for the continued support of the research or the particular researcher. The circumstances may be such that the only way to obtain the required sort of scientific results is by fraud—by claiming to have performed experiments with significant results when no such experiments were per-formed or no such results obtained. Scientific frauds are sometimes perpetrated in such circumstances; competent scientists, masters of the requisite practical knowledge, do things that are *at the same time* dishonest and bad scientific practice. A moral standard is violated and so, too, is a technical norm. A scientist knows that to commit such a fraud is a major sin. The tainted "results" not only fail to con-tribute to scientific knowledge; they detract from it. Other scientists may be misled by such falsehoods, perhaps to the detriment of their own work. The fraud poisons the well. The perpetrator shows a lack of proper respect for the aims of science and for colleagues whose work is thereby undermined. Both science and colleagues are sinned against.

6

Are there two distinct and independent norms, one scientific and the other moral, that indicate truthfulness in science? Or is there a single standard here, one that is at once scientific and moral? On the one hand, it would seem that a dedication to the aims of science and to excellence in scientific research, together with an under-standing of the importance of truthfulness in the practice of science, would be sufficient for a firm commitment to truthfulness in re-search. The requirement of truthfulness in science can be viewed as a technical norm, a directive that gets its authority from the charac-ter of the practice of scientific inquiry and the concerns peculiar to this activity.

To view the norm of truthfulness in science as a technical norm in this way is not to view it as what Kant called a "hypothetical impera-tive."[13] The norm does not say to the researcher, "If you happen to want to advance the purposes of science, then be truthful in your de-

13. In *Grounding for the Metaphysics of Morals*, Kant says, "[Hypothetical Impera-tives] represent the practical necessity of a possible action as a means for attaining something that one wants. . . . The categorical imperative would be one which rep-resented an action as objectively necessary in itself, without any reference to an-other end." The translation is by James W. Ellington in *Immanuel Kant: Grounding for the Metaphysics of Morals* (Indianapolis, Ind.: Hackett, 1981), p. 25.

scriptions of your work," with the understanding that if the researcher cares more about something else incompatible with the purposes of science, then the direction to be truthful is withdrawn. The researcher who desperately needs significant results now to secure a grant renewal may be willing to forgo advancing the general purposes of scientific research in order to secure support. The norm of truthfulness in science, however, indicates that this researcher's contemplated fraud is wrong. Its wrongness is not dependent upon the researcher's particular desires and purposes; it depends, rather, upon the activity of science and the concerns and interests that this activity serves.

Truthfulness is also a moral norm, but, as such, its authority has a different source from the authority of the technical norms of science. Presumably its source is to be found outside of the practice of scientific inquiry. Truthfulness as a moral norm belongs to a different realm of practical knowledge that somehow applies to scientific inquiry and many other activities. Two distinct norms—one moral and the other technical—indicate truthfulness in scientific research.

It is possible to take account of the case for regarding truthfulness in science as indicated by two different norms without embracing the idea that the source of the authority of the moral norm is radically different from that of the technical norms. The source that is external to the activity of scientific inquiry, upon which the moral requirement of truthfulness depends for its authority, is simply a great many *other activities*. Truthfulness is necessary quite generally in cooperative activities that require communication among participants. Scientific inquiry is simply one such practice. That people can generally be trusted to be truthful is a condition of communication; that people should tell the truth is a norm of communication. That this standard applies widely in our lives reflects the fact that the phrase, "cooperative activity involving communication among participants," describes most, if not all, important human practices and activities. It applies to a very prominent and pervasive feature of human life. What prevents an Immanuel Kant from willing that his maxim in lying should become a universal law is that this law would clash with a norm necessary for activities involving communication. The abortive universal law "contradicts itself" because it purports to regulate such activities, while effectively negating a condition necessary for them.

7

Consider again the scientist whose grant will be renewed only if results of a certain significance have already been obtained. Unfortunately, the results so far are disappointing. Suppose this scientist, however, is so committed to proper scientific procedure that lying about the results is not an option. So, the scientist describes the results truthfully, and the grant is not renewed. Is such scientific integrity different in kind from moral integrity? The proper contrast here would be a scientist in the same circumstances whose motive for rejecting the temptation to exaggerate the significance of the results and reporting them truthfully is honesty and an abhorrence of lying.[14] There is a reason for preferring the latter sort of person to the former. The individual who is committed generally to honesty can be counted upon to observe norms of truthfulness in a wide range of activities, including, of course, scientific research. Such a person has come to value truthfulness for its importance in a number of practices, and has developed the propensity to extend and adapt this norm quite generally to any activity involving communication. To the extent that the first scientist's truthfulness is motivated only by a commitment to norms of scientific inquiry, we cannot be as confident that this individual will observe norms of truthfulness in other areas. So, for example, if both scientists are candidates for the post of scientific advisor to an agency of government, we have better reason to think that the second individual will be an honest public servant than we have in the case of the first. Apart from this difference, however, there is no reason to suppose that the motivation of the honest person to avoid scientific fraud must be radically different from that of the scientist governed by standards of good scientific practice. Kant claimed that the truthful behavior of an honest individual has a motive and worth of an altogether different kind from the motive and worth of a truthful action of a

14. For purposes of contrast, each of the scientists is assumed to have but one motive for being truthful in this and the following discussion. This perhaps unrealistic assumption is necessary for expository purposes.

dedicated scientist observing a technical norm.[15] It is this claim, I think, that is not borne out.

In attempting to show that the ordinary understanding of morality is reflected in the central ideas of his philosophy, Kant drew our attention to phenomena such as an act of morally praiseworthy honesty—the sort of honest act that has "moral worth"—that is, an act that reflects credit upon the agent as an honest individual.[16] Such an act must have a certain sort of motivation. Acting honestly simply to maintain a reputation for honesty or out of love for those affected by one's action is not strictly the sort of action that expresses the virtue honesty. The latter sort of act is done from a special motive—one we know well, but which we have difficulty describing. The truly honest person acts honestly because it is wrong to do otherwise—period. Honesty is the firm determination to avoid this sort of wrongness, simply because it is wrong. This is not to be understood as a simple aversion or as an obsessive attachment to a taboo or as a quaint religious observance. Rather, Kant explains, we are to understand this as a respect for "law." Where norms exist for good reason in the affairs of rational beings, they acknowledge and respect these norms, insofar as they are reasonable individuals, even when the norms oppose their particular desires and inclinations. Acting honestly "from duty" is a matter of accepting the guidance of a certain norm out of respect for the norm.

This account seems to me correct and illuminating, as far as it goes. I want to add that the attitude toward norms that Kant tries to describe is necessary for there being norms at all, and so it is necessary for the existence of all kinds of activities and practices. This attitude is frequently exemplified when people are guided by technical norms. Acting from respect for a norm is not exclusively a "moral" phenomenon, in the narrow construction Kant placed on the term. Unlike Kant, I want to ascribe the existence and authority of all norms, including moral norms, to their roles in practices and activities.

The phenomenon that Kant called a "good will" is best understood by considering what is involved when an individual under-

15. Kant sharply distinguishes "technical" from "moral" imperatives in chapter 2 of the *Grundlegung zur Metaphysik der Sitten* (1785). The extraordinary origin and authority of moral norms is stressed throughout the work.

16. This, of course, is the announced purpose of chapter 1 of the *Grundlegung*.

takes to participate in a practice. Normally, the person will develop a cultivated concern with the purposes of the practice, and will accept the guidance of the norms of the practice, the standards by which the person's pursuit of the practice is judged to be good or bad. The individual, then, is concerned with practicing in accordance with the standards, on the understanding that by so acting, an agent flourishes in the practice and the practice itself flourishes in that performance. In this spirit, practitioners act in certain ways simply because it is right to do so, because it would be wrong practice to do otherwise. We might call such conduct "acting from respect for norms." Kant's account of a "good will" can be understood as a description of a commitment to respect in a similar way certain moral norms.

Kant described moral norms as having a special source and authority, different from technical norms. On his account, the motivation to observe these norms of an agent having a good will is different from the motivation to respect the technical norms of a practice. Kant viewed the sort of observance of moral norms that reflects moral credit on the agent as acting from respect for moral law, where moral law is described as universal, unconditional commands of reason. It is important to note, however, that when Kant argued that reason categorically prescribes certain laws, his argument frequently turns upon the plausible claim that certain important practices are impossible without those norms.

A better account, I think, would identify a "good will" with an agent's commitment to actual practices, including the internal purposes of the practices and the relevant norms. The agent would be committed to the simultaneous guidance of a multiplicity of norms relevant to the activity, in the light of their relation to the purposes of the activity and their relation to other practices. This attitude is to be contrasted with that of an individual who is determined to observe a certain standard—say, truthfulness—no matter what the consequences. In this case, norms are regarded as isolated commands to be obeyed blindly, without consideration for their interaction with the purposes and other associated norms of a practice. Besides suggesting a model of right action that represents it as the opposite of intelligent and sensitive, this sort of moral absolutism cannot deal with practical problems involving conflicts of considerations. On the more satisfactory account of "good will," the agent is guided by a standard *in relation to other standards* applicable to a practice. The agent understands and is responsive to the aims of the practice, the place and importance of other standards in its pursuit, and the relations of the practice to the social life in which it exists.

8

Normally, we learn about truthfulness as children in domestic and educational domains, where nurture and learning are dominating considerations. The "common life" in these spheres requires communication, and the importance of truthfulness here provides our first lessons with this item of practical knowledge. Because truthfulness will be required in other spheres, it is commonly taught as a "moral" requirement—one of wider application beyond the family and school. Precisely how the requirement applies in combination with the norms of other activities, however, must be learned in learning the *other* activities. So, for example, childhood lessons about truthfulness do not, by themselves, equip one to understand the distinction between the sort of hyperbolic claims in a scientific grant renewal proposal that might be viewed as acceptable "puffery" and those that constitute lying about one's project. In different domains of activity, one must learn how to follow a moral norm such as truthfulness (or beneficence, or fairness, etc.) in conjunction with the other norms that pertain in the particular domains, where various other interests and purposes predominate.[17]

It is important, then, to qualify in the following way the claim that morality is a body of practical knowledge analogous to medicine and agriculture. What we call "morality" appears to be a collection of practical considerations that are important in many practical do-

17. Some of us are taught as children that moral norms are absolute commands that are to be followed without question. The way that we are taught about lying and truthfulness sometimes militates against our intellectual apprehension of the importance of adjusting our understanding of the requirement of truthfulness in new practical domains. For an account of the actual cost of the acceptance of Augustine's teaching that a lie is always and absolutely wrong, see Jonsen and Toulmin, *The Abuse of Casuistry,* chap. 10. The price historical events exacted for this doctrine was paid both in moral confusion and in human suffering.

mains. These considerations, taken together, do not define a particular domain of activity on all fours with medicine or family life. They are not in that sense a "body." They are, rather, abstracted from particular domains on account of their frequency of occurrence and their general importance, and, for a variety of purposes, placed together on a list. The abstracted considerations and norms, as a group, are not structured by any particular activity, so they are not ordered in a way that indicates their relative priority when two or more of them conflict in a concrete situation. Their ordered structure emerges only in particular practical domains, where a learned activity is pursued in accordance with its particular group of norms, including relevant moral norms.

Practical knowledge, including moral knowledge, involves knowing how to observe simultaneously a cluster of norms, and the constituents of such a cluster invariably change from one practical domain to another. It is not surprising that there are no algorithms for harmonizing moral norms in the abstract. The absence of algorithms for harmonizing the moral norms that pertain in a particular practical domain is no more remarkable than the absence of mechanical decision procedures for medical practice, scientific research, or family life. The world in which we practice changes, and our knowledge and interests change in response. The life we share through our shared practical knowledge and interests continually encounters problems, some of them unprecedented. We must create ways of coping. Success in leading the life we share, where we achieve it (we are not always successful), is partly a matter of improvisation, of adapting our norms and purposes in response to novelty. This is perhaps the supreme test of intelligence.

9

To understand any sort of norm, it is necessary to understand how it functions together with other norms in one or more practices. If among the norms of a certain body of technical practical knowledge are some that are recognizable as moral norms, then an understanding of that moral norm as it pertains to that particular practice will involve an understanding of the practice. In fact, moral norms are common among the norms of complex practices. Because this is so, there is such a thing as an ethics that pertains to a particular practice, an ethics that requires for its developed understanding an understanding of that practice. The ethics of professions such as medicine, law, education, and engineering are examples of ethics pertaining to specific practices.

A variety of professional organizations in areas such as law, engineering, health, and business have formally adopted written codes of professional ethics.[18] Such organizations often have more than one reason for this exercise. Sometimes ethical codes are conceived as primarily disciplinary—professionals prefer to police themselves rather than being regulated from outside. In order to afford due process to those subject to the code, it is thought necessary to have an explicit written code of conduct. The code then has a quasi-legal function, and its adoption is, at least in part, an attempt to preempt formal legal regulation. Such codes, however, are also thought of as having ethical authority. They exist in order to inform and guide members of professions in the conscientious performance of their professional activities. The code might fulfill this second educational function even if the organized profession did not formally enforce its provisions by punishing violators. Different professions vary in the relative importance that they attach to the regulatory and educational functions of their professional codes.

A particular code of professional ethics would consist of a list of formulations of some of the norms pertinent to the professional activity. The norms would be selected for various reasons; the particular selection, however, would be a reflection of the ethical problems the members of the profession and others regard as important for its activities. Thus, it might be possible to draw conclusions about the state of a profession and its relationship to its clients and community at a certain time from the professional code of ethics it promulgated.

Some view codes of professional ethics, conceived as contributions to ethics, as otiose: After all, these skeptics argue, professional groups have no power to create moral principles. At best,

18. See, for example, the Code of Ethics for Engineers of the National Society of Professional Engineers in Gorlin, *Codes*, pp. 69–74.

such groups can formulate already existing moral principles. Such principles, however, will not be specific to any profession but will be familiar general moral principles that apply to all activities. It would be better to think of this as just ethics rather than some special ethics pertaining to a particular profession.[19] This skeptical view, however, fails to take account of the facts that moral norms are found among the technical norms that pertain to the practice of professions and that an understanding of how moral norms function with respect to that activity requires an understanding of the activity itself.

In the course of defending the importance of a code of professional ethics for the field of engineering, Michael Davis proposes that existing formal written codes are attempts to express what it is to "think like an engineer."[20] Davis emphasizes the cooperative character of professions organized to promote members' pursuit of the goals of the profession. The principle that engineers in the performance of their duties "hold paramount the safety, health, and welfare of the public" is a central tenet of several formal codes of engineering ethics. Engineers adopt (i.e., create) this principle as a sort of "convention," Davis argues, in order to protect themselves from certain pressures from clients and others to "cut corners" (153–54). When clients, in order to save time or money, urge engineers to compromise the safety of a project, a convention among engineers to make safety paramount protects engineers from the threat that they will be replaced if they do not compromise their standards. Engineers adopt this convention by formally articulating it as a principle of professional ethics. They are obligated to follow this principle of engineering ethics by the "principle of fairness": because an engineer "accepts the benefits of being an engineer . . . , he is morally obliged to follow the (morally permissible) convention that helps to make those benefits possible" (160). Without this convention and the resulting obligation to other professionals, an individual would

---

19. See John Ladd, "The Quest for a Code of Professional Ethics: An Intellectual and Moral Confusion," in *AAAS Professional Ethics Project*, ed. R. Chalk, M. S. Frankel, and S. B. Chafer (Washington, DC: AAAS, 1980), pp. 154–59.

20. Michael Davis, "Thinking like an Engineer: The Place of a Code of Professional Ethics in the Practice of a Profession," *Philosophy and Public Affairs* 20.2 (1991), 150–67. Numbers in parentheses in the text refer to pages in this article.

have no basis "as an engineer" to object to unsafe projects. Any reservations would be "personal" rather than professional (158).

One of Davis's aims in this account is to refute the claim that since genuine moral obligations exist independently of the actions of professional organizations, codes of professional ethics are superfluous. Davis's strategy depends upon the general point that people can create moral obligations by means of tacit or explicit undertakings or agreements. He argues that professions in their cooperative practices create "conventions" in order to aid one another in pursuing professional goals, thus creating moral obligations to one another specifically as professionals. These "conventions" constitute a special set of moral obligations that are incumbent upon members of a profession as such; they constitute a code of professional ethics. This code may be written down and formally adopted by a profession, but such formal procedure is not necessary for its existence as a code.

The basis of some tenets of professional ethics no doubt are due, partly or wholly, to a convention among professionals of the sort that Davis describes. Engineers, as such, however, have obligations directly to clients and to the public that are not merely the result of their obligations to fellow professionals. The requirement cited by Davis—that engineers make paramount the safety of the public—is an example of an obligation of engineers to the public. When engineers design an unsafe bridge, their failure is not just in their responsibility to other engineers. The public has standing to claim that they themselves are wronged by engineers who design unsafe artifacts. It is doubtful, then, that the requirement that engineers make safety paramount is based entirely upon some sort of contract engineers have made with one another.

There is, however, an important point in engineers' publicly affirming their professional obligation to make safety paramount, and their (as it were) covenanting with one another to observe this norm. Besides the regulatory and educational function of such joint action, engineers thereby help one another to resist pressures to compromise such standards by affirming the standard and making public their collective determination to abide by the standard. An engineer who yields to pressures to cut corners not only fails in an obligation to the public but also lets down other engineers.

Davis uses events leading up to the disastrous 1986 explosion of the space shuttle *Challenger* to illustrate the extraordinary pressures that are brought to bear on engineers to compromise the safety and welfare of the public. Engineers at Morton Thiokol, Inc. (MTI), who had designed the solid rocket boosters that lifted the *Challenger* into space, had known for more than a year that the rubber O-rings that seal the boosters' segments lose their resiliency as the ambient temperature decreases. Should the rings fail, pressure, heat, and flame would escape from the joints, and the shuttle would explode. Tests had shown that at 50 degrees Fahrenheit, these seals were unreliable. The day before the *Challenger* disaster, a temperature of 30 degrees was forecast for the Cape Canaveral launch site the following morning. The evening before the scheduled launch, the MTI engineers recommended against launch, on the grounds that it was not safe at the expected temperature. NASA officials argued against the recommendation to postpone the launch on the grounds that the engineers did not have sufficient proof that the projected launch was unsafe. NASA wanted to launch on schedule, and MTI managers (some of whom were engineers) overruled the recommendation of their own engineers. The shuttle was launched the next morning. It exploded shortly after take-off, and all seven astronauts aboard died.

The responsibility for the *Challenger* disaster does not fall only on the MTI engineer-managers who, despite their awareness of serious doubts about the safety of the launch, approved it under pressure. NASA was anxious to prove the commercial potential of the space shuttle by demonstrating that it could be depended upon to fly on schedule. After the glory days of the moon-landing project, NASA's funding had been reduced; what funding there was had been pried from Congress by promising feats of space flight with the space shuttle that were unrealistic. The insistence on safety that had prevailed in the projects leading up to the moon landing had been relaxed in the attempt to produce with reduced funds a cost-efficient space shuttle that could eventually pay for itself.[21] That the MTI engineers needed every support to resist the extraordinary pressures brought upon them to compromise safety in the circumstances of

21. See Nicholas Carter, "The Space Shuttle *Challenger*," in *Ethics and Politics*, ed. Amy Gutmann and Dennis Thompson, 2d ed. (Chicago: Nelson-Hall, 1990), pp. 117–28.

the space shuttle program is manifest. The enormous pressures that government agencies and large corporations can bring to bear upon conscientious individuals to act wrongly are truly daunting. That engineers should need to covenant with one another to stand firm and support one another against pressures to compromise in their work the safety and welfare of the public is readily understandable in the light of this example. To act competently to realize the purposes of their profession, engineers need to be able to make effective their particular trained outlook with its characteristic concerns. The *Challenger* disaster illustrates the cost of a failure of this outlook properly to influence a decision that obviously should have been informed by it.

Davis describes the professional goal of engineers as the "efficient design, construction, and maintenance of safe and useful objects" (153). An *unsafe* bridge, automobile, or space shuttle is, for that reason, a badly engineered product. Engineers who do not make paramount in their work the safety of those who use their products and of the public generally will thereby diverge from norms of excellence of engineering practice. One cannot care about building bridges well and be indifferent to whether people can use these artifacts safely. Bridges that deliver people to the other side of obstructions broken in body and spirit are not good bridges. Engineered products that enable users to accomplish their purposes well and safely but which are detrimental to the health and safety of people other than the users are apt to violate norms of community life.[22]

The principle that engineers hold paramount the safety, health, and welfare of the public does indeed express an important point about what it is to "think like an engineer." The practical knowledge that is the province of engineers is organized around the goal of designing safe and useful artifacts. Besides knowledge of the physical sciences and an understanding of what levers to move to make specific things happen in the world, engineers characteristically have certain concerns. These concerns are not extraneous additions to en-

22. Safety is compatible with a reasonable assumption of risk, but what risks are reasonable is a complicated matter. Safety in, say, infants' furniture, automobile travel, parachutes, and experimental space craft are in a way obviously (and properly) different from one another. For a discussion, see Charles Fried, *An Anatomy of Values* (Cambridge: Harvard University Press, 1970), part 3.

gineering knowledge—the concerns organize and structure engineering knowledge; they are an integral part of such knowledge. Such concerns provide the rational basis for the standards of proper procedure in engineering, the norms of good and bad work in engineering. Learning to be an engineer is not just a matter of absorbing information—it involves internalizing the concerns and standards that order that body of practical knowledge. Thinking like an engineer will reflect certain concerns and priorities, and chief among these will be the design of safe and useful artifacts. This will be a central feature of thinking like an engineer whether or not engineers, as a group, make it a practice to support one another in their pursuit of this goal.

That the safety of users of artifacts is part of the defining goal of engineering practice, it will be objected, does not establish it as an ethical principle that engineers make safety paramount; this renders it only a technical rule. Consider, though, why the defining goal of engineering is the design of artifacts that are useful, efficient, and safe. The interests of people that are served by this goal are the reason for the existence of the activity of engineering. The effective promotion of this goal makes an important contribution to the life of the community. Engineering is an important profession, and it is conceived as it is, with the defining goal that it has, because of the general interest among members of the community in having certain artifacts that are, among other things, safe and useful.

It is helpful here, too, to think of a community as Plato does in *Republic*, Book 2: A certain division of labor among citizens contributes to a relatively self-sufficient community that provides its citizens with much that they need in order to live and flourish. People work full time at specialized tasks for which they are suited, and so arts, crafts, and professions are cultivated and developed. For the citizens and the community to flourish, these practices must be pursued effectively and harmoniously. Plato called the state of affairs in which citizens pursue their different work effectively and harmoniously "justice" (*dikaiosune*) in a "community" (*polis*). Pursuing successfully the profession of engineering as a part of such a social scheme is noble and important.

A code of ethics of a profession will properly stress the community's interest in the defining goal of the profession, including the concern that the professional activity be pursued effectively with a minimum of interference with other important pursuits and interests. The principle that good engineering practice conduces to the design of safe and useful objects is a technical norm, a norm of proficiency of the profession of engineering. It is at the same time a corollary of the more general social norm, the ethical norm, that important work should be pursued effectively and harmoniously. The general norm is an important and intelligent convention of the community; it is this norm that gives citizens standing to complain when those who undertake to do the work of engineers fail to produce safe and useful artifacts. A proper code will articulate certain engineering principles that are also ethical principles. Such norms exist in the nature of the particular practice; they do not depend upon the practitioners' agreeing with one another to support one another in upholding them. At the same time, it is reasonable for professionals to covenant to support one another in confronting the pressures they will encounter to depart from those norms.

It is well said, then, that the codification of the ethics of the profession of engineering is an attempt to express central features of what it is to think like an engineer. Central concerns of engineers that structure the body of practical knowledge that is their province will reflect not only their mutually supportive practices, but also the interest of the community in what they do that is the source of their work and the basis of their claim that the work is important and worth doing. Practical knowledge in general is inseparable from concerns about what can be done with the knowledge. Morality, as practical knowledge, is inseparable from certain very general interests and concerns.

6. Activity and Distributive Norms

1

Consider norms that pertain to the distribution of things. In the course of our myriad activities, it falls to us, together and as individuals, to distribute, collect, bestow, withhold, impose, and waive a great many things. It is often a matter of the greatest importance *how* such things are done, and there are norms that we appeal to in determining the appropriateness of a certain distribution. I want to explore the idea that the norms by which distributions are properly evaluated are themselves determined by the character of the activities that occasion the distributions and by the purposes of the people engaged in those activities. How far are the norms that govern the distributions that belong to a specific activity conditioned by the activity itself? The answer is: to a very considerable extent.

Activities are many and varied. If the norms by which distributions are properly evaluated are substantially determined by the activity that occasions the distribution, then we would expect that quite different modes of distribution would be appropriate for different activities. This indeed is what we find. The sorts of norms of distribution that philosophers have in mind when they discuss distributive justice appear to be various, often conflicting, and it is a standard philosophical project to find and articulate what it is that gives justice its "unity." Chapter 5 of John Stuart Mill's *Utilitarianism* is an example of such an undertaking.

Nicholas Rescher lists seven "canons" of distributive justice, each canon being a principle based upon a different type of consideration that can be relevant to establishing the validity of a claim for a share in one sort of distribution or another. Proponents of rival theories of distributive justice, Rescher says, tend to focus upon one or another of these canons to the exclusion of the others. So, different and competing accounts are based upon the exclusive selection of just one of the following ways of completing the sentence:

Distributive justice consists

wholly or primarily, in the treatment of all people:

1) as equals. . . .
2) according to their needs.
3) according to their ability or merit or achievements.
4) according to their efforts or sacrifices.
5) according to their actual productive contribution.
6) according to the requirements of the common good. . . .
7) according to a valuation of their socially useful services in terms of . . . supply and demand.[1]

Each of these theories is based upon *a* consideration that grounds claims for shares in certain distributions, but each is mistaken, Rescher says, in denying the validity of claims based upon the *other* six considerations. He offers the following alternative:

Distributive justice consists in the treatment of people *according to their legitimate claims*, positive and negative. This canon shifts the burden to—and thus its implementation hinges crucially upon—the question of the nature of legitimate claims, and of the machinery for their mutual accommodation in cases of plurality, and their reconciliation in cases of conflict. To say this is not a criticism of the principle, but simply the recognition of an inevitable difficulty which must be encountered by any theory of distributive justice at the penalty of showing itself grossly inadequate.[2]

1. Nicholas Rescher, *Distributive Justice* (Indianapolis, Ind.: Bobbs-Merrill, 1966), p. 73.
2. Ibid., p. 82.

Although Rescher's seven canons do not exhaust the types of considerations that do, from time to time, ground claims for shares in distributions, he has listed seven important types. What is striking, of course, is the multiplicity of these considerations, their variety, and the obvious potential for conflict among them. The questions of when claims based upon one or another of these canons are legitimate and how their reconciliation is accomplished are central.

2

Alasdair MacIntyre attributes conflicting views about what justice dictates in particular distributions to cultural malaise and theoretical disorders. The various conflicting claims that are made in the name of justice are, on his view, based in historically different moral traditions. We possess the ideas of these various claims in the form of fragments torn from the historical social contexts that gave them meaning. These claims, as a result, are not altogether intelligible to us, MacIntyre says, and it is not surprising that we have no rational method for resolving conflicts among them. "Our pluralist culture possesses no method of weighing, no rational criterion for deciding between claims based upon legitimate entitlement against claims based upon need. Thus these two types of claim are . . . incommensurable, and the metaphor of 'weighing' moral claims is not just inappropriate but misleading."[3]

The hypothesis that differences in norms of distribution are determined by differences in the activities that occasion the distributions provides an alternative to MacIntyre's explanation of the diversity of these claims. If the conflicting claims are based in different activities, and if we are simultaneously engaged in more than one activity or in a single highly complex activity, then the fact that we recognize conflicting claims as reasonable and relevant is not necessarily a sign of cultural and intellectual disorder. Rather, a certain amount of diversity and conflict is just what we should expect, especially in a community that cultivates many different activities in the pursuit of a variety of interests. Should a certain activity attain a sufficient de-

---

3. Alasdair MacIntyre, *After Virtue*, p. 246.

gree of complexity, so that it has aspects of or similarities to more than one sort of established activity, then it would not be surprising to discover, as we do, that conflicting distributive principles find a basis in what people are doing. In most cases, the social contexts that give these principles meaning are not lost to us in the remote past. They are immediately before us in the complex activities that we have mastered. This is not to deny, of course, that some disagreements about the appropriateness of a given norm to a certain distribution are due to the sort of causes MacIntyre cites.

People do tend to fasten upon a single distributive norm and attempt to apply it quite generally, without considering various paradigms of actual distributions where the norm uncontroversially legitimates claims and others where it does not. Their conflicting "intuitions" are often vague recollections that their favored norm has proved authoritative; they do not attend to the details of when and why it was authoritative. When parties to a dispute about a particular distribution have fastened in this way upon different norms, a resolution of the dispute is difficult, as long as they persist in viewing the norms as they do. People often have sharply conflicting interests at stake in distributions, and they tend to choose principles that favor their private interests and favorite causes. Aristotle noted such disagreements: "Most men, as a rule, are bad judges where their own interests are involved. . . . but there is also another reason—they are misled by the fact that they are professing a sort of conception of justice, and professing it up to a point, into thinking that they profess one that is absolute and complete."[4]

Among disputes about distributions we find examples of what Michael Walzer calls "the common experience of moral disagreement—painful, sustained, exasperating, and endless."[5] Such disputes often instance one or more intellectual disorders, but such disagreement is not peculiar to our culture.

It is true that we do not possess *a* method, a *single* procedure, for properly deciding among conflicting claims for distributive shares, but it does not follow from this that we are without intellectual means for resolving such conflicts. There is not *a* method for treating

4. Aristotle, *Politics*, 3.9, 1280 a 15–23. The translation used is that of Ernest Barker, *The Politics of Aristotle* (Oxford: Clarendon Press, 1948), p. 117.
5. Michael Walzer, *Just and Unjust Wars* (New York: Basic Books, 1977), p. 11.

illness or for explaining difficult points in the classroom, either; rather, there are a variety of ways of healing and teaching that people have learned, and there are many techniques adapted to the effective solution of various sorts of problems that arise in the course of pursuing these activities. We are more or less successful in solving various medical and pedagogical problems; sometimes, however, such a problem defeats us altogether. Of course, unprecedented problems encountered in these pursuits may lead to disagreements about which of the many ways that have proved useful with past problems should be employed. In view of the complexity and variety of problems of healing, pedagogy, and conflicting claims in distributions, we should not expect a single method of problem-solving for any of these areas.

This appears to be MacIntyre's problem in another form: How are we to decide with a problem about distribution which of these many ways is properly employed? This question is apt to arise if the problem is difficult and the issues involved are controversial. Of course, we do not have "a method" for deciding such matters. It would be a mistake, however, to conclude that either we must find a single method or abandon all hope of intelligent resolutions. The *particular* problem whose solution we seek typically will yield to some approaches and not to others. Some of the techniques that are more or less effective with the particular problem will interfere with other things while other effective techniques do not or do so to a lesser extent. The nature of the particular problem and the context in which the problem occurs often will determine which approaches offer better or worse solutions. This same point extends to problems about how certain things are properly distributed. A careful attention to the nature of the activities that occasion the particular distribution, to the purposes of the people engaged in the activities, and to the relationship of the proposed solutions to the larger social context may provide compelling reasons for preferring one solution to another.

We cannot say in general—in the abstract—how to weigh claims based upon entitlements against claims based upon needs. It does not follow, however, that we have no rational way of resolving conflicts among such claims in particular circumstances. What we lack is a way—any way—of doing this in the abstract. We have no way, apart from a relatively concrete situation that involves the pursuit of specific activities and purposes, of determining the relative importance of different practical considerations. On the hypothesis that norms of distribution, activities, and purposes are interrelated, this result is neither surprising nor discouraging.

At least some of the many norms by which distributions are properly evaluated are importantly relevant to the various philosophical conceptions of justice. Philosophical accounts of the standards of distributive justice, however, sometimes neglect the crucial connections of those standards to their social contexts and the myriad shared activities that comprise those contexts. As a result, the familiar standards viewed from certain of these perspectives take on an altered aspect. These formulations preserve in certain respects the outlines of the phenomena they are intended to characterize and illuminate, but essential features are omitted. The standards described more or less in isolation from the activities to which they apply lack features that are important for understanding their application, and so the descriptions neglect matters crucial to understanding the norms. They are indeed fragments torn from the historical social contexts that give them meaning. To understand a practical consideration is to know how to apply it *together with other considerations* in the intelligent conduct of one or more activities. The attempt to explain a practical consideration such as a norm of distributive justice in abstraction from the activities to which it applies effectively separates the explanandum from matters essential for its intelligibility. Certain philosophical accounts of justice separate norms of distribution from the social and historical contexts that give them meaning. There is a remedy, though, in attending carefully to those contexts.

It is apparent that an adequate understanding of any norm or standard will involve a knowledge of how to apply it. How a standard is properly applied, however, will be governed to a considerable extent by what it is being applied to. An essential component of our understanding of how certain things ought to be distributed is our ability to apply the relevant standards in actual situations and to deal in a reasonable way with the sort of problems that arise in such applications. So, for example, to understand the principle that in a distribution of things of a certain kind, allotments should be determined in such a way that certain needs are fulfilled as far as possible, it is necessary to know specifically what sorts of distributions, things, and needs are meant. One also needs to know how to apply this principle together with other applicable norms. Locking swine in houses and burning the houses to the ground may be an effective way of producing roast pig, but it is an insane procedure, given the cost and importance of houses. We understand norms in clusters in relation to their simultaneous application to one or more activities.

3

William Frankena's classic article "The Concept of Social Justice" illustrates nicely some of the difficulties encountered when principles of distribution are abstracted from the activities to which they apply.[6] In this brief discussion, Frankena compiles a list of criteria for a society's being just. A just society, according to Frankena, has written or unwritten rules so that it treats similar cases similarly. A second requirement for a just society is that it treat people equally unless there is a special kind of justification for treating them differently. A just society, Frankena says, respects certain differences among people, including differences in capacity and need and in contribution, desert, or merit. There are then a number of principles, similar to Rescher's "canons," directing that people be treated differently on the basis of such things as capacity, need, and merit. Frankena suggests that these principles can be thought of as qualifications of the principle of equal treatment. The principle that agreements should be kept, Frankena says, is another principle that qualifies the principle of equal treatment. Further, a just society does not injure, interfere with, or impoverish its citizens, even when in so doing it would be abusing its citizens equally and impartially (13–14). A just society, then, conforms to principles of (1) regularity and impartiality; (2) equality of treatment; (3) difference of treatment in certain cases of difference in capacity, need, and merit; (4) fidelity to agreements; and (5) non-interference and non-injury.

6. William K. Frankena, "The Concept of Social Justice," in *Social Justice*, ed. Richard B. Brandt (Englewood Cliffs, N.J.: Prentice-Hall, 1962). Unless otherwise indicated, page numbers in parentheses in the text refer to this work.

These principles are norms that are at least arguably relevant to questions of distributive justice. They seem a motley collection, however. Frankena asks, echoing Mill, what relates these principles of justice? (14). We think of justice as in some important way a single feature of societies and other things. Yet these principles seem more or less different and distinct. In what does their unity consist? It does not seem that any norm pertinent to distributions is ipso facto a norm of justice. How are these principles of justice different from other norms of social ethics, such as principles of beneficence and utility? Why are these particular principles requirements of *justice*, while other principles of social ethics are not?

So far, the formulation of these principles and the claim that a just society fulfills these principles is too abstract and general to be a satisfactory account of these matters. Indefinitely many social arrangements—including some unattractive ones—might satisfy all of these requirements under some plausible interpretation or other. The requirements Frankena lists often conflict with one another when we attempt to apply them in concrete cases. It is decidedly not our view that when such principles conflict, it does not matter how the conflict is resolved. Many of the most difficult problems concerning distributions involve conflicts among requirements such as these, and we expect that an understanding of these norms will enable us to devise defensible solutions to such problems. It is important, then, that an account of justice say something about the interpretation and the application of these principles, and this will require attention to the relationship of these principles to one another. It is important to address the problem of the unity of justice. The account should indicate how we are to go about answering such questions as: When do differences in individuals' needs justify departures from the principle of equality? When does the principle of equality permit the state to interfere in the lives of its citizens? When are we justified in departing from the principle of regularity and impartiality in order to fulfill a hitherto unnoticed claim based upon desert? And so on. What is missing, here, is any indication of how these norms are applied together to particular cases.

Frankena's answer to the question of how these different requirements of justice are related to one another is that they all express a concern that each individual live as good, as fulfilling a life as possible. The concern is an egalitarian one, he says, because it is directed equally at every individual. Here are his words:

> A just society, then, is one which respects the good lives of its members and respects them equally. A just society must therefore promote equality; it may ignore certain differences and similarities but must consider others; and it must avoid unnecessary injury, interference, or impoverishment—all without reference to beneficence or general utility. The demand for equality is built into the very concept of justice. (19–20)

So the requirement that people be treated equally and the requirement that certain differences among people be respected merge into a single requirement of equal treatment: People should be treated equally except where there are compelling reasons for unequal treatment. Individuals differ in their needs and capacities for living a good life, so an equal concern for their good living should recognize the appropriateness of different treatment in some cases. Sometimes, then, different treatment will be required in order that individuals' equal chances for a good life be enhanced in the long run. The principle of equal treatment should be understood in this light.

The idea that the norms of social justice express an equal concern for the good of each individual is attractive; it articulates a central ideal of egalitarian democratic political morality, and we resonate to it. This characterization of the focus of the norms of social justice, however, does not suffice to provide the desired account of the relation of these norms to one another, the account that will guide the application and reconciliation of these norms. The principles, even in the light of this egalitarian purpose, remain abstract and vague. One of Frankena's examples in his discussion of the principle of equality illustrates the problem:

> So far treating people equally has been equated with treating them similarly or in the same way. But suppose that society is allotting musical instruments to C and D, and that C prefers a banjo and D a guitar. If society gives C a banjo and D a guitar it is treating them *differently* yet *equally*. If justice is equal treatment of all men, then it

is treatment which is equal in this sense and not simply identical.
. . . It is hard to believe that even the most egalitarian theory of justice calls for complete uniformity and not merely substantial equality. (11)

What, though, is the difference between treating C and D differently and equally and treating them differently but *not* equally? It
won't do for Frankena's purposes, as he realizes, to equate treating
people *equally* with treating them in the *same way*. Note that we treat
C and D in the same way in as much as we:

—give each the same kind of musical instrument.

—give each the instrument she prefers.

—give each the instrument she needs.

—give each an instrument whose name begins with the letter 'b.'

—etc.

It is apparent that in one and the same action we might treat C and
D in exactly the same way in some of these respects and not in the
same way in others. Indeed, it may be impossible to treat them in the
same way in all of these respects. It is also clear that there are indefinitely many ways in which we might treat C and D in the same way
in allotting musical instruments to them, and it is most unlikely that
in one particular distribution we can treat individuals alike in all
ways.

Treating people equally, according to Frankena, is treatment that
shows an equal concern for the chances for a good life of each.
Sometimes such a concern properly leads us to treat people in the
same way and sometimes it requires us to treat people differently.
Suppose, though, C prefers a banjo and D a guitar, but both need a
guitar if each is to become as proficient as possible in playing such
instruments. (Assume that C and D know how to play neither instrument and that music teachers recommend that beginners learn
to play the guitar before they take up the banjo.) What in this case
would constitute treating them equally in giving them an instrument? What distribution would best promote the chances for a good
life of both C and D? Is it even reasonable in this case to use the

equal-treatment principle, understood in this way, to decide who gets which instrument?

It is not clear how to answer these questions. With more information about the case, we might form a judgment about what would constitute treating C and D appropriately in giving them musical instruments, but it is by no means clear that treating them appropriately will turn out to be the same thing as treating them equally, that is, treating them with an equal concern for the good life of each. The mode of distribution that constitutes appropriate treatment will differ considerably from case to case, depending upon what is being allotted and also upon the purpose for which it is distributed, what people will then go on to do with what is allotted.

We do not have enough information to decide which way of allotting instruments to C and D would be appropriate, and whether the appropriate allocation is in some sense equal treatment. We need to know why they are being given these instruments. What is going on? Not enough background of the proper sort is supplied to enable us to decide the question.

4

The following example supplies some of the background missing in Frankena's example of distributing musical instruments; the example also illustrates how the character of an activity and its purposes determine the way in which certain benefits and burdens should be distributed in connection with it. It is apparent in this example that an activity has a determinate character that quite effectively indicates certain modes of distribution and rules out others.

Suppose we have a warehouse full of assorted musical instruments, and we are charged with distributing them in order to start an orchestra. We could treat everyone in the same way by giving each exactly the same kind of musical instrument, but this is obviously preposterous. To insist upon this sort of equality of treatment would defeat the purpose of the distribution—forming an orchestra. The setting of the distribution, the nature of the things distributed, and the shared purpose of the people involved rule out giving each person the same instrument. Should the people be treated in the same way by giving them the instruments they want to have, the instrument that they prefer to play? First of all, the feasibility of this proposal depends upon the preferences that these people actually have. If everyone wants to play the drum, this will not be a satisfactory basis for distribution in this instance. Ingenuity might enable us to overcome this difficulty. We might give people an equal chance to play the instruments they prefer by drawing up a list of how many instruments of each kind are needed in the orchestra and establishing an order of choosing among the people by drawing lots. This would give the recipients an equal chance to receive the instruments they prefer to play. In some circumstances, this might be a reasonable way to proceed, but it may or may not be appropriate in this imaginary case. It is important to know why these people are forming an orchestra. Are they committed to giving a concert next week? Do they aspire eventually to become a world-class orchestra? If the answer to either of these questions is "yes," then the proposal that instruments be allotted by chance is a foolish one. What is obviously indicated in some circumstances is a system of distribution that will place instruments in the hands of those who are skilled or who are apt to become skilled at playing them. The suggestion here that instruments be distributed in such a way that each recipient has an equal chance to live as well as possible is not a useful one. The purpose proposed for the distribution by the suggestion is too vague, too unspecific, and the sorts of considerations it gestures at are of doubtful relevance.

People might have other purposes in forming an orchestra, and different purposes would indicate different modes of distribution of instruments. An orchestra's purpose might be educational, recreational, ceremonial, or therapeutic. It would then be reasonable to take into account in allotting positions in the orchestra such things as people's preferences, certain of their needs, their aptitudes, their skills, or their accomplishments—depending upon exactly what the purpose of the orchestra is. It might be reasonable for them to devise a way of distribution that takes account of more than one of these things. Once again, it is apparent that the nature of the activity that occasions the distribution and the purposes of the people involved determine to a considerable extent what mode of distribution is appropriate. In these cases, too, Frankena's principle that things be distributed so that each individual has an equal chance to live as good a life as possible is too unspecific and of doubtful relevance.

It is also apparent that if the people forming the orchestra are not in agreement about the purposes of their undertaking, they are apt to encounter difficulty in agreeing about the appropriate way of distributing instruments. To the extent that we lack a shared understanding of the activities we undertake together—to the extent that we disagree about the purposes of various modes of social cooperation—we will find it correspondingly difficult to agree about how to distribute the benefits and burdens whose distribution these activities occasion. Our discrepant purposes will tend to indicate different, incompatible modes of distributions, and, as long as our purposes are different, it will be hard for us to agree about distributions. To reach the conclusion that, in general, we lack any way to adjudicate disputes about competing claims pertaining to distributions, however, we would need the premise that we disagree quite generally and extensively about the purposes of our activities *and* the premise that there is no way to resolve such disagreements. Neither of these premises is compelling.

Important features of these homely examples are to be found in many actual situations in which questions arise about the proper way to distribute something. In such cases, how things should be distributed depends substantially upon some very particular and concrete circumstances, including the nature of the things to be distributed, the sort of activity that occasions the distribution, and the purposes of the people engaging in the activity. What an orchestra *is* plays a central role in determining how people should proceed in establishing one; what an orchestra *is* is determined by the complex activity of making music, an activity that can have a number of purposes and a variety of standards by which it is done well or poorly. This is further complicated by the fact that there are different kinds of music and orchestras. Given the existing understanding of music and orchestras, it will be possible for people to have importantly different purposes in organizing orchestras and making music, but these activities in the particular forms in which they exist will limit the purposes people can have in forming orchestras and the ways in which they can adapt orchestras to their own purposes. Of course, there is left considerable room for differences of purpose and disagreement about modes of distribution. In analogous ways, the activities in the course of which people distribute various other things provide a logical structure for the practical situation that indicates certain ways of proceeding as reasonable and others as unreasonable, including modes of distributing things.

5

Michael Walzer, in *Spheres of Justice*, argues that distributive justice is substantially determined by historical and cultural circumstances.' Distributions are properly guided by the "social meanings" of the things distributed, Walzer maintains, and such meanings are created by the shared ideas of a group of people at a given time and place. There is a plurality of goods whose social meanings dictate a plurality of distributive principles. "Distributions are patterned in accordance with shared conceptions of what goods are and what they are for" (7). "If we understand what it is, and what it means to those for whom it is a good, we understand how, by whom, and for what reasons it ought to be distributed" (9).

When he states his position generally, Walzer does not emphasize the role that people's activities and practices play in their shared conceptions of goods and how these are properly distributed. In his discussions of particular goods and distributions, however, the decisive importance of complex activities emerges. For example, he says: "When medieval Christians . . . condemned the sin of simony, they were claiming that the meaning of a particular social good, ecclesiastical office, excluded its sale and purchase. Given the Christian understanding of office, it followed—I am inclined to say, it necessarily followed—that office holders should be chosen for their knowledge and piety and not for their wealth. There are presumably things that money can buy, but not this thing" (9).

Given the "meaning" of holy office—which includes a conception of the functions of the office (what holders of such office *do*)—allotting such positions solely on the basis of the candidate's ability to

7. Michael Walzer, *Spheres of Justice* (New York: Basic Books, 1983). Unless otherwise indicated, numbers in parentheses in the text refer to pages in this book.

pay makes little sense. The people who are served by the holders of such office have grounds for complaint when such offices are treated simply as commodities to be bought and sold (143–47). To embrace the idea that piety and knowledge are *not* of paramount importance for priests would have involved such extraordinary changes in the Christian church as it existed at the time that it is hard to know what would be left of the institution. Qualification, in the form of knowledge and piety, is indicated as a basis for the distribution of such office by the very nature of the office. The character of the activities that are the role of ecclesiastics determines what is qualification for such office, and these matters are determined by the practice of a particular religion.

When the United States first instituted a military draft in 1863, there was a provision that allowed a man whose name was drawn in the draft lottery to purchase an exemption from military service for three hundred dollars. Such exemptions led to deep resentment, since these enabled the rich to avoid risking their lives in the Civil War, while citizens who lacked the cash were required to face the awful dangers of battle. No such exemption was permitted in the United States in later wars. Walzer says of this example: "The state could not impose a dangerous job on some of its citizens and then exempt others for a price. That claim spoke to a deep sense of what it meant to be a citizen of the state—or better, of this state, the United States in 1863. One could make the claim good, I think, even against a majority of the citizens, for they might well misunderstand the logic of their own institutions or fail to apply consistently the principles they professed to hold" (99).

The burden of the defense of this egalitarian democratic state and the personal risks entailed properly fell equally on all able-bodied men as a duty of citizenship; the possession of three hundred dollars and the willingness to trade this sum for an exemption bore no reasonable connection with the duties of citizenship, particularly the waiving of the duty to risk one's body in battle in defending the state. The political life of the country, with its norms and purposes, properly understood, effectively ruled out such an exemption from a duty of citizenship. The activity, here, is a complex one—it is civic activity in a particular state. Just as certain rights and benefits are to be enjoyed equally by members, certain burdens are to be shared equally.

Citizens are to share such burdens as defense equally, but this does not imply that every citizen must be a warrior. Those who are not "able-bodied" are exempted from military service, because their ability to defend effectively is reduced and the burden of the effort would presumably be much greater for them than for the able-bodied. Women, too, have been exempted from military conscription, presumably for similar reasons. It would be a mistake today to exempt women from a military draft on the grounds that they are not qualified for military roles and that such service would be excessively burdensome for them. Even so, it still might be that the exemption of women in the Civil War was justified. War and military service were different in the nineteenth century, and so was the part women played in civic life.

6

An example of an actual distribution problem of considerable complexity is the allocation of places in a kidney dialysis program when such a medical resource is in short supply. In the 1960s, when the technology for renal hemodialysis was new, the number of patients with severe kidney ailments who needed such treatment in order to live far exceeded the available places in treatment programs.[8] The ways in which this scarce medical resource was actually allotted have been much discussed and criticized. An obvious and paramount consideration in allotting places in a medical treatment program, indicated by the nature of the practice of medicine, is medical need.[9] In this case, however, the number of individuals who could claim treatment based upon medical need was much greater than the number who could be treated. It was not enough in this case simply to treat those whose need was greatest, because there was a superfluity of patients whose medical need was as great as possible—they needed renal dialysis in order to live. Their claims based upon medical need were very strong and equal in strength in the

8. David Sanders and Jesse Dukeminier, Jr., "Medical Advance and Legal Lag: Hemodialysis and Kidney Transplantation," *UCLA Law Review*, 15.2 (1968), 357–413. See p. 366.
9. See Walzer, *Spheres of Justice*, chap. 3, especially pp. 86–91.

sense that each patient in effect was saying, "I need this treatment in order to live; if I am denied treatment, I will die."

In situations in which the number of individuals needing treatment exceeds the available medical resources, medical people consider, in addition to medical need, the likelihood of successful treatment. So, for example, if two patients need immediate lifesaving treatment and only one can be treated at a time, the patient whose survival with treatment is doubtful would be treated after the patient whose prospects of recovery with treatment are good. There are, then, at least two distinguishable principles of triage: (1) Treat patients in order of medical need, and, (2) Use scarce medical resources first where they are reasonably expected to be more effective, where treatment is more likely to be successful. It is obvious that these two principles are grounded in the nature of the activity of healing, the practice of medicine.

The second principle—the principle of effectiveness—applies in the case of selections for a hemodialysis program. If the number of applicants with the greatest medical need—those who need dialysis in order to live—exceeds the number who can be treated with limited resources, then there is a strong case for using the available resources as effectively as possible. That is, patients should be chosen in such a way that as many lives as possible can be expected to be saved. The problem presented by the scarcity of dialysis in the 1960s was severe because those not chosen would almost certainly die as a result. In such circumstances, it is particularly urgent to use the available resources as effectively as possible, to save as many lives as possible. The thought that such precious resources might be wasted and lives lost that might be saved is deeply disturbing. The principle of effective use is clearly applicable. From among the superfluity of patients needing dialysis in order to live, it is appropriate to select first for treatment those whose prospects of successful treatment are relatively good.

In fact, however, these two principles were not the only ones used in the early days of hemodialysis. Apparently, the number of applicants needing hemodialysis in order to live whose prospects of successful treatment were relatively good exceeded the number of patients who could be accommodated. In a widely publicized case, the Seattle Artificial Kidney Center of the University of Washington established a committee of anonymous citizens whose charge it was to select candidates for dialysis from a group who had been determined to be self-supporting citizens of the State of Washington, under forty years of age, and medically suitable. This committee, according to reports, made the final selection based upon social and economic criteria. They favored applicants who were solid citizens with a record of public service and individuals with dependents. As David Sanders and Jesse Dukeminier, Jr., noted, the committee considered such factors as "age and sex of patient; marital status and number of dependents; income; net worth; emotional stability, with particular regard to the patient's capacity to accept the treatment; educational background; nature of occupation, past performance and future potential; and names of people who could serve as references."[10]

The operation of this committee was criticized for the lack of explicit selection criteria and for the idiosyncratic character of some of its selections. "The descriptions of how this committee makes its decisions, published in *Life* and *Redbook*," wrote Sanders and Dukeminier, "are numbing accounts of how close to the surface lie the prejudices and mindless clichés that pollute the committee's deliberations. . . . The magazines paint a disturbing picture of the bourgeoisie sparing the bourgeoisie, of the Seattle committee measuring persons in accordance with its own middle-class suburban value system."[11]

Three different but related criticisms of the operation of the committee need to be distinguished. One criticism is that in determining the "social usefulness" of the applicants, the committee used an unacceptably narrow conception of social usefulness, neglecting, among other things, the roles of those who support unpopular causes. ("The Pacific Northwest is no place for a Henry David Thoreau with bad kidneys.") A second criticism is that it is simply not possible to rank people according to their social worth—how does one determine the relative usefulness of a lawyer, a grade-school teacher, a poet, and a stone mason? How are these to be compared? ("Selection of patients by ad hoc comparisons of social worth

10. Sanders and Dukeminier, "Medical Advance and Legal Lag," p. 377.
11. Ibid.

is objectionable.") Finally, there is the objection that the selection of patients for treatment in such a circumstance, where failure to be selected means death, should not be done on the basis of judgments of "social worth" at all. This objection is based upon the idea that for purposes of determining how lifesaving treatment is to be allocated, all human lives should be regarded as equally valuable.

The view that social worth should be taken into account in allocating scarce lifesaving resources, according to James Childress, "would in effect reduce the person to his social role, relations, and functions. Ultimately it dulls and perhaps even eliminates the sense of the person's transcendence, his dignity as a person which cannot be reduced to his past or future contribution to society."[12] Childress advocates a two-stage selection process in which, first, candidates are eliminated from consideration who fail to meet certain criteria of medical acceptability. Then assuming that the number of remaining applicants still exceeds the number who can be treated, the final selection is made by a random procedure such as a lottery. The rationale of the random procedure is that it gives each candidate who is medically acceptable an equal chance to receive lifesaving treatment. Unlike a selection procedure that uses criteria of social worth, the random-selection procedure is thus compatible with the assumption of the equal value of the life of each applicant.

There is an important objection to Childress's argument. If we have several individuals who need a certain medical treatment in order to live, he argues, their claims to receive treatment are equally strong. If we cannot treat all of these individuals, we should not choose the recipients on the basis of their superior social usefulness, because this is contrary to the supposition that their lives are equally valuable. It is this claim that is doubtful. Obviously, if we are to choose between things that are alike in a certain respect, then we cannot use the respect in which they are alike as the grounds for choosing between them. It is not inconsistent with noting this likeness, however, to choose one over the other on the grounds that in *another respect* they are *not* alike. If two musical instruments produce sounds of equal quality, a musician, recognizing this similarity, might choose

12. James F. Childress, "Who Shall Live When Not All Can Live?" *Soundings* 53.4 (1970), 339–55. See p. 346.

one rather than the other because it is easier to play or because it is more durable. To choose one fine instrument over another because of its ease of playing is not inconsistent with the knowledge that the two instruments produce sounds of equal quality.

Given the purpose of the practice of medicine, every patient who can truthfully say, "I need renal dialysis in order to live," has a very strong claim to receive treatment. Their claims are equally strong, however, and, therefore, if it is necessary to choose some but not all for treatment, the selection cannot be made on the basis of this medical need. Another ground needs to be found for making the selection. Childress assumes that the *only* ground that is consistent with our recognition of the equality of their claims based upon medical need is a random-selection procedure that gives each an equal chance of receiving treatment.

To see that Childress's assumption is mistaken, suppose someone actually did propose that scarce places in a kidney dialysis program be distributed to those needing the treatment in order to live *solely* on the basis of a lottery, no other considerations whatever being consulted. On this proposal, all those who need this treatment would have an equal chance of receiving it. Probably no one has ever proposed such a thing; the proposal is open to the following obvious objection. Among those needing renal dialysis are individuals whose prospects of being successfully treated are significantly better than others. A selection procedure based upon nothing but a lottery would be less likely to distribute treatment to those with better prospects of successful treatment than would a procedure designed to allocate treatment to those most likely to respond satisfactorily. This is a very serious defect of the simple lottery procedure; it is of the greatest importance that scarce lifesaving resources be used as effectively as possible. In circumstances where the need exceeds the available resources, it is disturbing to think that any of the scarce resource would be wasted. The case for using the principle of effectiveness here is strong. If the principle is used, however, not everyone who needs dialysis in order to live will have an equal chance of receiving treatment. From among equally needy patients, those will be selected who have the greatest chance of being successfully treated, in an effort to ensure that as many patients as possible are saved. Such a procedure in no way denies the equal importance of the claim of each applicant to need the treatment in order to live.

Most people who have thought about this problem will agree that it is important to use what I have called the principle of effectiveness in such a selection. Childress, for example, countenances the use of such a principle in the "first stage" of the selection procedure when candidates who are "medically suitable" are selected. The importance of the rationale for the use of the principle of effectiveness here is that it suggests a way of justifying *other* principles of selection, including some of those put in the category of considerations of social worth. In the event that the number of "medically suitable candidates"—those who need dialysis in order to live *and* who have a relatively good chance of being successfully treated—is still larger than the number who can be accommodated, Childress argues, the equality of candidates' claims based upon medical need requires that each be given an equal chance to receive treatment. Suppose, though, that some of the "medically suitable" candidates are parents with young dependent children and others have no dependents. A procedure that ensured that these parents were among those selected for treatment would be preferable to one that left this to chance; the same number of medically suitable people would be treated on either selection procedure, but the former procedure would be more likely to provide for certain dependent children than the random selection.

With the defense of the use of the principle of effectiveness in mind, we can defend in the situation described selecting certain patients with young dependent children over those without dependents. The claims of all applicants based upon medical need are strong and equal in force; where the number who can make this claim exceeds the resources for treatment, the selection cannot be made on the basis of *this* consideration. The two-stage selection procedure favored by Childress (select "medically suitable" candidates and then choose from this group by lottery the number that can be accommodated) will satisfy the principle of effectiveness, but it will not address the needs of dependent children for a parent as reliably as a system that assures that parents are selected for treatment. It is not necessary to claim that patients with children are for that reason more worthy or deserving of being saved in order to defend selecting those patients; we are not weighing the lives of applicants in

some kind of value scale and finding some individuals more deserving, some lives more worthy of preservation than others. Rather,
we seek a way of selecting from among a group of applicants whose
lives are equally valuable, whose claims on the basis of medical
need are equal, and whose prospects of successful treatment are relatively good. We propose a system of selection that not only enables
us to serve as effectively as possible the medical needs of patients as
far as the scarce resource permits, but which also enables us to serve
the needs of certain dependent children as well. The selection system Childress advocates cannot be expected to serve the needs of
dependent children as reliably as one that favors parents. We prefer
the latter system because, besides serving the equal claims of patients as well as the alternative, it also more effectively addresses the
important needs of certain *other* individuals who are immediately
and profoundly affected by the selection.

One might challenge the assumption that dependent children
have important needs that *only* a particular parent can fulfill; if the
assumption is exaggerated or untrue, the argument for considering
dependents in allocating lifesaving treatment is undermined. Even
if the assumption can be sustained, it is no doubt true that some parents in fact do not fulfill these important needs of their children. If it
is not feasible for the allocators to determine which of the parents effectively fulfill their children's needs, it still might be arguable that
important needs are addressed by an allocation system that favors
parents with dependent children. A certain rough imperfection is
sometimes unavoidable in these procedures.

There is nothing in this rationale that denies or conflicts with the
idea that every applicant needing dialysis in order to live has a
strong and equal claim to receive treatment. The rationale is based
upon the argument that where the number of applicants for treatment exceeds the resources available and where their claims based
upon medical need are equal, we should favor allocations that, in
addition to fulfilling the medical needs of as many patients as possible, address at the same time important needs of other individuals affected by the selection. Of course, physicians have a special
responsibility, grounded in the character of their activity, to address
medical needs of patients; normally, when the medical needs of a
patient conflict with needs of another party who is not a patient, the

physician properly gives the patient's medical needs priority. Physicians, as such, are not immediately concerned to serve young children's needs for nurturing; a physician who favored parents for dialysis because of the needs of their children would not thereby be treating those children as patients. In this case, however, there is no conflict between treating as many medically needy patients as possible and addressing important needs of certain dependent children. A physician can simultaneously practice good medicine and beneficence and good citizenship. Provided that selecting a system that also serves important needs of dependents will not interfere with the most effective use of resources to address as effectively as possible the medical needs of patients, it is appropriate for medical people to consider the needs of those who are not patients. As they practice medicine, they are also taking part in the larger life of the community.

7

The claims for renal dialysis of patients who need the treatment in order to live and whose prospects of successful treatment are good are very strong and equal. If there are more patients with such a claim than can be accommodated, then some other basis than these patients' medical need must be found for selecting those for treatment. One possible basis is to consider the important needs of individuals other than the applying patients. To select for treatment a patient whose treatment addresses important needs of others is not to deny that this patient has no stronger claim based upon need than any other patient. Once the argument against "social worth" considerations based upon the equality of claims of patients is rejected, it is apparent that a wide variety of considerations might reasonably be taken into account in the allocation of scarce lifesaving resources. Nicholas Rescher propounds and defends such a scheme.[13] His allocation procedure, too, involves two stages, the first stage eliminating whole classes of applicants by means of what he calls "criteria of in-

13. Nicholas Rescher, "The Allocation of Exotic Medical Lifesaving Therapy," *Ethics* 79.3 (1969), 173–86. Unless otherwise indicated, page numbers in parentheses in the text refer to this article.

clusion." This is followed by a second stage in which the remaining applicants are compared on a case-by-case basis using "criteria of comparison" to make the final selection (175).

Among the criteria of inclusion, besides those designed to eliminate from consideration patients whose prospects for successful treatment are low, Rescher discusses what he calls the "constituency" and the "progress of science" factors (176–77). The constituency factor is based upon the fact that medical treatments are often available from institutions that have an identifiable constituency—for example, state hospitals, veterans' hospitals, children's hospitals. Depending upon how the constituency is constituted, it may be defensible in cases of scarce lifesaving treatment to give priority to individuals who belong to the constituency of the institution providing the treatment. So, for example, the Seattle dialysis selection committee considered only applicants who were residents of the state of Washington, on the grounds that since the treatment facility was supported by state funds, citizens of the state should be its primary beneficiaries.

The progress of science factor depends upon the fact that there may be important medical research interests that can be pursued by treating classes of patients who fall into a certain category—children, diabetics, individuals with a negative Rh factor, and so on. Where the pursuit of a particular line of research in conjunction with the treatment of a certain group of patients promises to benefit future patients, the argument—that a selection procedure that allocates treatment to this group is, other things being equal, preferable to a procedure that does not—is straightforward.

The argument for taking into account a constituency factor, as the Seattle committee did, is based upon the fact that besides dispensing medical treatment in the course of practicing medicine, the Seattle committee is also dispensing a resource that belongs to the state of Washington and, in a way, to the citizens of that state. This resource, by its very nature, answers to very important needs of individuals, needs of a kind for which the state already makes provision. So, for example, when individuals in the state of Washington are unable to provide for themselves food and shelter essential to life, the state undertakes to provide these things. It is one of the perquisites of citizenship that the state has a particular obligation to make provision for citizens. This is not to say that only citizens are eligible for such provision, but when there is not enough for every needy person, citizens properly have a stronger claim upon state resources than noncitizens. Citizens of a community have special responsibilities toward one another, such as the duty to make provision for certain important needs of those citizens who are unable to provide for themselves. Provisions are properly made for the security and welfare of visitors, but a citizen, as such, has special claims. This is connected with the point and value of being a citizen, what makes citizenship a good.[14] As a state medical facility, the Seattle Hospital is engaged in practicing medicine, in contributing to medical knowledge, *and* in making provision for certain needs of the members of the polity.

In a second stage of the selection process, Rescher proposes to rank particular cases using criteria of comparison such as the relative likelihood of successful treatment, the patient's life expectancy with successful treatment, the patient's family responsibilities, the patient's potential for future contributions to society, and the patient's past contributions (177–79). By these criteria, not only is an effort made to maximize the number of patients treated successfully in the sense of preventing their death from a specific condition, but in addition an effort is made to maximize the number of years of life for the recipients of the treatment. In this respect, a young patient with good prospects of being restored to good health after treatment is to be preferred to an elderly patient whose life expectancy even with successful treatment is considerably shorter. This may have been the reason why the Seattle committee considered only applicants who were under forty years old. Taking age into account in this way can be defended on the grounds that more good is done in an obvious way by preserving thirty years of life than by preserving five years of life. It will be objected that it is unfair to deny someone lifesaving treatment on grounds of age, but the fact is that the elderly have already lived most of their life and younger people have not. The quality of life of an elderly person, moreover, is apt to be less good than that of a younger person. Of course, anyone of any age has a very strong claim on a medical resource that the individual

14. On this see Michael Walzer, *Spheres of Justice*, chap. 3.

needs to live. If we are forced, by scarcity of resources, to choose between saving an elderly person and a young person, it is defensible on the grounds offered to save the younger person.[15]

Rescher's proposal to consider in this sort of allocation such matters as the patient's past contributions to society and prospects for future contributions is problematic. Taking the promise of future contributions into account could be defended on the grounds that important needs of people who can be expected to benefit from these contributions are thereby taken into account. If the head of state is among the superfluity of candidates for lifesaving treatment during a period of national crisis, the case for including the leader among the recipients might be compelling. This is not because political leaders are more deserving of treatment than others, but rather because many people need the services of this person; *their* claims are compelling. On the other hand, if one takes seriously the idea of ranking all applicants according to the importance of their expected future contributions to others, the task is truly daunting. It is often difficult to predict what contributions an individual will make. There is not, moreover, a single defensible ranked list of what the community's most important needs are.

Medical treatment is not a prize to be awarded for merit, so it may seem strange to propose that lifesaving treatment be allotted as a reward for past services to society. There are cases, however, where this sort of consideration clearly has force. For example, it is reported that when meager supplies of the new drug penicillin were delivered to U.S. forces fighting in North Africa in 1943, army doctors proposed to use the drug to treat the battle-wounded. They were overruled at higher levels of command, however, and the penicillin was used to treat soldiers with venereal diseases, on the grounds that these soldiers could be returned to action more quickly.[16] It is natural to feel that the battle-wounded were more deserving of treatment; they, after all, had risked their lives and health

15. Daniel Callahan employs a similar argument in making a case for allocating health care, excepting comfort care, first to those who have not yet completed a normal life span. See *Setting Limits: Medical Goals in an Aging Society* (New York: Simon and Schuster, 1987).

16. Henry K. Beecher, "Scarce Resources and Medical Advancement," *Daedalus* (Spring 1969), 279–80.

in defense of their country and had been wounded in this service. Their country was indebted to them, and their claim for scarce life-saving treatment was strong. This is surely right, and the justification for allocating the drug elsewhere was, perhaps, that the battle was still in doubt and that every soldier who could be thrown into the fight might be important to the outcome. As a result, unfortunately, some deserving wounded would die. The latter were soldiers too, however, and their commanders were sacrificing them in the war effort in much the same way that they were sacrificing the troops in the front line who would be killed in action.

In cases where a certain individual's survival will fulfill some clear and urgent social need, the argument for allocating that individual scarce lifesaving treatment will have force. Similarly, where society's debt to someone is unusually great, this might become a serious consideration in the case for allotting scarce lifesaving treatment to the individual. In the case of a group of individuals who have during their lives been in various ways contributing members of the community, however, it will often be infeasible to assess the relative importance of their contributions—past or prospective—for the purpose of a defensible selection procedure for scarce lifesaving resources.

Rescher's response to an allocation problem in which there is a plurality of defensible considerations is not to seek a selection procedure that attempts to satisfy just one sort of consideration. After all, there are other considerations, and any procedure that dismisses all considerations but one will be open to the objection that it does not take account of the considerations dismissed. Rescher seeks ways to use as many of them as possible in the selection. The rationale for this is that a selection procedure that satisfies more defensible claims is, so far, better than a procedure that satisfies fewer. A selection procedure should take account of as many relevant considerations as possible, but, as Rescher emphasizes, there is likely to be more than one way of doing this. If certain considerations are taken into account, the situation may dictate that other considerations cannot be taken into account. There are apt to be various ways of weighing the relevant claims and considerations that are defensible and feasible. There will be better and worse ways of proceeding, but there is not necessarily a single optimal way of combining these considerations. Rescher calls this the "nonoptimality" of selection systems (182–83). Often, to be effective, lifesaving treatment must be applied quickly. Should it turn out that an allocation procedure that takes account of many relevant considerations takes so long to implement that applicants are apt to die before the selection can be made, it is obvious that such a procedure is unacceptable. Medical need is paramount here, and treating patients who are apparently medically suitable on a first come, first served basis may often be the best procedure that the circumstances allow. The feasibility of taking account of a certain arguably relevant consideration is a crucial matter in designing a defensible allocation procedure.

8

Certain renal dialysis programs in the 1960s were *at once* medical practice, scientific inquiry, and community provision for important needs of citizens. The discussion of the allocation of scarce places in dialysis programs illustrates the way in which activities having important multiple aspects can produce circumstances in which many different norms of distribution are arguably relevant. Those applicants who are allotted places in a program will live longer as a result, and those who are refused will die sooner. The scene is thus set for difficult problems about how lifesaving resources are to be distributed in connection with such activities. Various more or less reasonable claims for shares in the distribution are bound to conflict, and the question of how properly to respond is painful and difficult. It would be misleading to describe the source of the problem here as "theoretical and cultural disorders": complexity of activity, plurality of considerations, and the ensuing conflicts of considerations encountered in practice are not necessarily social malaise. Such problems indicate that our intellectual resources require extension and reorganization, but the genesis of the problems may be discovery, innovation, and growth. Our discussion of such problems sometimes evidences misconceptions about the considerations or about practical reasoning generally; in this way, philosophical disorders hamper us in resolving conflicts.

The discussion of the dialysis problem also indicates the importance of what Rescher calls the "nonoptimality" of any selection system. In circumstances where there are many different distributive norms that are relevant, there may be several different distributive schemes that respond adequately to most or all of the relevant claims to shares in the distribution. The schemes may clearly be among the better ways of proceeding, but there may not be one scheme among them that is *the* right way of allocating things, the others being wrong ways. Scheme A may be better than scheme B in one respect but inferior to B in another respect. It may not be clear which respect is more important. The example challenges the assumption that there is a super-norm called justice that trumps all the other norms and dictates a unique solution to any distribution problem. Conflicts of distributive norms and the nonoptimality of any selection system are the result of the plurality and complexity of activities, norms, and purposes, and of Heraclitus's principle that everything flows, that novelty and change are continual.

The multiplicity of relevant norms and the nonoptimality of allocation schemes is common in concrete distribution problems. Consider controversies about taxation, about various ways to distribute the burden of raising monies for the activities of government. J. S. Mill, in Chapter 5 of *Utilitarianism*, discusses an argument for taxing everyone the same amount, on the grounds that people should be charged the same sum for the same privileges, whether they can afford it or not.[17] The rationale for this scheme is the analogy with other contexts where we expect to be charged a fixed fee for a privilege or a service—club dues, mess privileges, bridge tolls, and so forth. Mill suggests, of course, that we reject this scheme for reasons of "humanity and social expediency," but other important differences between citizenship and club membership or crossing a bridge are not hard to find. We could just as well argue that requiring everyone to pay the same sum for taxes does not distribute equally the *burden* of financial support of the state. Citizenship in our egalitarian democratic state means citizens' sharing equally in certain civic burdens as well as civic rights and benefits. Similarly, it is commonly argued that a flat-rate income tax imposes unequal burdens on citizens, since it is easier for the rich than for the poor to

---

17. John Stuart Mill, *Utilitarianism* (Indianapolis, Ind.: Bobbs-Merrill, 1957), pp. 71–72.

part with the same percentage of their income. From the standpoint of equalizing the burden, a graduated income tax is thought to be better than a flat-rate tax. The idea is to equalize the "pain" of paying an income tax, but the goal is imprecise and the success of efforts to achieve it are hard to assess. Presumably, we must tolerate rough imperfection here too. Still, it seems to us important to make the effort—one's fair share is an equal share of the burden. The principle of citizens' sharing equally in the burden of paying taxes is obviously not the only norm that pertains to such allocations. Various schemes of taxation attempt to reduce the size of the difference between rich and poor, to encourage contributions to charity, to make it easier for people to own their own home, to stimulate investment, to encourage the purchase of municipal bonds, and so on. The sale of tobacco and alcohol is highly taxed, partly on the rationale that users of these products are apt to make greater demands on healthcare resources. One reason for the complexity of many of our systems of taxation is that we attempt in them to respond to many reasonable considerations, but these schemes are open to the criticisms that they are so complex that they are unreasonably difficult to administer, that they are wasteful and inefficient, and that the response to one consideration tends to undermine the attempts to respond to others. The thesis of nonoptimality clearly pertains here; there is no such thing as *the* just system of taxing income or alcohol and tobacco.

The nature of our purposes and the activities associated with them, together with the concrete circumstances in which we pursue these matters, are crucial determinants of how things are properly distributed. This will hold for the distribution of various burdens, benefits, opportunities, honors, privileges, and offices that people distribute collectively—as a community. This point will hold, then, for what John Rawls calls "social justice"—"the way in which the major social institutions distribute fundamental rights and duties and determine the division of advantages from social cooperation."[18] Frankena, of course, did not claim that the principle of equal treatment is a determinant of the appropriate mode of distribution

18. John Rawls, *A Theory of Justice* (Cambridge: Harvard University Press, 1971), p. 7.

in *every* sort of case. His claim is that this is a principle of *social* justice. This means presumably that it governs the way in which a society should distribute the things that it is its business to distribute.
Even this claim, however, is too strong. We may establish a national
orchestra or a state dialysis center, but the question of how instruments or positions in such an orchestra are to be allotted or how the
medical treatment is to be distributed would properly be determined by the sorts of considerations we have already discussed. The
precept that things be distributed in such a way that everyone has
an equal chance to lead a good life is not useful in these latter discussions. In the cases where something like the principle of equal
treatment is an important determinant of how things are properly
distributed, we should expect to find that it is the nature of the public activities of a community and the shared purposes of its members
that account for the relevance of the principle.

9

In Book 3 of the *Politics*, Aristotle discusses how political powers
and offices should be distributed in a *polis*. Various distributive
schemes are evaluated by considering their appropriateness in the
light of political activity and its purpose. Something like Frankena's
principle of equality, in the form of a claim about the purpose of the
political association, plays a central role in the argument. Aristotle
maintained that communities exist because human beings are natu-
rally social, because they need a community in order to live, and because community is necessary for good living. The good life, he said,
is the chief end of both the *polis* and the individual (1278b 15–30).[19]
Although he did not explicitly say that the purpose of the polis is
that *each* individual member have an *equal* chance to live as well as
possible, he endorsed the view that political power is properly exercised in the interest of *all* of the ruled (1279a 7–21).

This view plays a crucial role in his argument. The discussion pro-
ceeds by an examination of the soundness of the rationales offered

19. References in parentheses in the text are to the Bekker edition. The translation used is that of Ernest Barker, *The Politics of Aristotle*.

for various claims for shares of political power. The wealthy claim a monopoly of political power on the grounds that they possess the wealth of the community; the many poor claim that each citizen has an equal claim to a share of power on the grounds that each citizen is just as much a citizen as any other. There is a point to both arguments, according to Aristotle, but each argument is based upon an incomplete understanding of justice (1280a 7–1281a 10). When oligarchs and democrats put forward their competing claims in this fashion, they leave out of account the most important thing—the purpose for which people come together in a political association. What has the possession of wealth to do with the ability to direct the business of a *polis* in such a way that the purpose of a *polis* is advanced? If a *polis* were simply a business partnership or a trade association, the possession of property would be an indication of an individual's ability to contribute directly to the purpose of the association. A *polis*, however, is an association for the purpose of good living, of *eudaimonia*. A major element in good living is the exercise of excellences of character and intellect in a wide range of activities. How the offices in a *polis* should be allotted and how the power necessary to direct the business of a *polis* should be distributed needs to be considered in the light of the sort of activity that governing a *polis* is and the purpose of this activity. The oligarch must connect the peculiar "worth" (*axia*) of a property owner with the purpose of the *polis*, by showing how a certain amount of political power allotted to just such a person would contribute to that purpose, and the strength of the oligarch's claim must be weighed against the claims of others (1280a 20–b 12).

Similarly, the democrat who argues that office and power should be shared equally, because every citizen is just as much a citizen as every other, has not yet connected this sort of equality—which I assume is an equality of "worth" of a sort—and the distribution based upon it with the nature of the political association and the purpose of it. What has equal possession of citizenship to do with conducting the business of a *polis*? "The democrats believe that equality in one respect—for instance, that of free birth—means equality all around" (1280a 23–25)—including equality of "worth" that will sustain a claim to office and political power. A certain sort of equality, however, will argue that equal shares are appropriate only when there is the proper sort of connection between *that* sort of equality and the undertaking that occasions the distribution.

Aristotle considers the claim of the best people in a *polis* to rule; these presumably are the brightest, most able, most dedicated, most high-minded, most conscientious, most public-spirited individuals. Such people obviously make a substantial contribution to the life of the *polis*. They, moreover, are in a superior position to direct the *polis* effectively towards its end. They have a firsthand knowledge of excellence, and they have qualities important for directing the business of the *polis* effectively. A citizen's claim to office and power based upon the possession of such qualities as these is strong. Given the primary purpose of the political association, it seems reasonable to entrust the business of the community to these individuals who are best equipped to understand and to perform the activity of governing.

Aristotle recognizes merit in some arguments for the claim of the people at large to rule and not just the few best. The few best are not the only ones in the community who have good qualities; the people at large have a degree of understanding and character that is substantial. This should not be ignored. They can contribute to the intelligent direction of the community from their store of knowledge and experience. If moral and intellectual excellence is a reasonable claim to office and power, then the citizens as a whole have a claim based upon whatever excellence they possess. Simply to ignore this claim would be unjust. Since the possession of political office is a sort of honor (perhaps in the sense of a public recognition of their actual character and understanding), to ignore the claim of the many is to dishonor them. "A *polis* with a body of disenfranchised citizens who are numerous and poor," Aristotle reminds us, "must necessarily be a *polis* that is full of enemies" (1281b 29–31).

In response to Plato's argument that the best and brightest should have a monopoly of political power, Aristotle points out that if the many pool their knowledge and insight, they may on some matters be more likely to make sound political judgments than individuals who possess a degree of knowledge and political ability that is superior to the ordinary citizen's. If the many meet together as a deliberative body, the errors of individuals can be exposed by others, the insights of individuals can be combined, and the opportunity for individuals to pursue their own interests contrary to the *polis's* interests are diminished. Moreover, those who are not political experts but who live in the *polis* and with its problems may be aware of important things that the expert does not know. One of Aristotle's analogies here is the position of the client of an expert house builder and repairer vis-à-vis the question of how the client's house should be. The client has a body of experience of living day to day with the house, a firsthand knowledge of what the problems are and how serious they are. For the expert builder to ignore the client's special knowledge of how the house should be would be a mistake. It might be objected that this analogy does not work, because in the case where the expert builder is also a resident of the house, the builder has sufficient experience from the resident's point of view. The expert in *polis*-craft is also a citizen of the *polis* and has the citizen's perspective, so the experience of citizens who are not experts is superfluous. In a community where there is a division of labor and a variety of social roles, however, there is no such thing as the citizen whose experience exhausts all of the points of view that are relevant to and need to be taken account of in political decisions. It is reasonable, then, to conclude that a wide range of citizens have knowledge that is relevant to the proper conduct of the business of a *polis*, the fostering of good life for all. It is this knowledge that could emerge in a deliberative body made up of many citizens. If the possession of practical knowledge necessary for the successful conduct of the business of a community is an argument for political power, then the ordinary citizen has a sound claim for a share of political power. The precept that the purpose of the *polis* is to promote the good life of all its citizens is a central premise of the argument.

The political scheme that is indicated by Aristotle's discussion in *Politics* 3 is this: It is preferable to have the best and brightest in high political office. The ordinary individual citizen is more apt to go wrong in executing the duties of the office than is the outstandingly knowledgeable individual of extraordinary character and political skill. At the same time, however, the body of ordinary citizens would elect officials to high office, and officials would be formally answerable to the *polis* at large for their actions in office. Such a system would recognize the important insights of the ordinary citizens, it would provide rulers with an incentive to take account of the views of the many, and by not excluding them from political power, it would avoid alienating them.

In this discussion, Aristotle assesses the reasonableness of various individuals' claims to political power by considering how various ways of responding to those claims would contribute to the conduct of the business of the *polis* and the realization of the purpose of the *polis*. He says that a distribution of power and office will be just when it is allocated in accordance with the "worth" (*axia*) of each claimant. It would be consistent with his discussion to understand Aristotle to mean by an individual's "worth" for any given distribution those attributes of the individual and the individual's situation that are the basis for a reasonable claim to whatever is being distributed. In the discussion in *Politics* 3, what attributes ground a reasonable claim turn out to be determined by the character of what is being distributed and why it is being distributed, by the activities and purposes that occasion the distribution. In assessing the reasonableness of various claims in this discussion, he appeals to the nature of the *polis* and the nature of the activities that constitute living in a *polis* and conducting its business.

Aristotle recognizes a number of competing reasonable claims and understands the problem to be to find a way somehow to respond to all such claims. Given the claims that are found to be relevant, there may in fact be several ways of proceeding that respond to them all in some fashion. It is not necessary to assume that there is but one mode of distribution that constitutes a single correct solution to the problem as Aristotle sees it, all other solutions being wrong. There is no reason to suppose that Aristotle thought differently. Rather, there are better and worse schemes, with some of the better schemes being preferable for a variety of reasons, including ones that derive from the peculiar circumstances of a particular community. The better schemes, however, will reflect a concern for the good life of the members of the community.

Aristotle's approach to political justice and certain of his conclusions can usefully be adapted to our own political context. He offers an argument that supports what we understand as political democracy. The argument meets head-on Plato's impressive argument against democracy and shows that the latter argument's assumption that knowledge entitles a person to rule actually supports the claim of the ordinary citizen to take part in ruling.[20] Aristotle did not understand the argument to show that women who lived in a *polis* should share in its governance, at least partly because he believed that women lacked just the qualities of intellect and character that are the basis of an individual's claim to political power.[21] When the falsity of this belief is recognized, the argument sustains the claim of women for a share of political power on the same terms as men.

10

What, though, if someone rejects Aristotle's account of the purpose of the political association? Aristotle's view is that the *polis*, conceived as he conceived it, is a natural phenomenon, the outcome of the natural development of a human community when all goes well, the flourishing of a political association.[22] Different communities, however, have different experiences, different histories, different circumstances. Aristotle's notion that the best thing that could happen to any community is to turn into a *polis* is parochial. Whatever can be said in favor of Aristotle's conception of community as a natural phenomenon, a particular community is also a complex artifact, a way of life that consists in a system of activities, norms, and purposes that a group of people have developed over a long period of time. The saying that a political association exists for the purpose of fostering good living for all its members describes a political community as we understand it, and there is a great deal to be said for such an association.

Some will view the account, so understood, as unsatisfactory, however, precisely because it makes the appropriateness of designing modes of social distribution so that they foster good life for the members of the community contingent upon the forms of activities current in the community and in the purposes people in fact have in their activities. The claim that the rationale for norms governing distributions—including norms of distributive justice—is to be found

20. Michael Walzer makes a strong case for the importance of Plato's argument against democracy in *Spheres of Justice*, pp. 284–87.
21. See *Politics*, book 1, chapter 13 (pp. 33–38 in Barker).
22. See Barker's Introduction to *The Politics of Aristotle*, pp. xlviii–l.

substantially in the particular activities that occasion the distributions and the associated purposes is taken to imply that such norms lack a sufficient basis, that we cannot provide a satisfactory defense for these norms. It is thought that such an account will not be able to provide the desired sort of rational defense for norms of distribution because the basis of the rationale offered for the norms is too ephemeral, too contingent, too arbitrary.

If people adopted complex activities and purposes whimsically, if all practices and institutions were nothing more than fads, then perhaps there would be a certain arbitrariness about all activities that would infect any norms internal to the activities. In fact, though, there is a notable absence of well-founded historical explanations of existing activities that attribute these substantially to caprice or accident. The more important activities that are available to us typically were occasioned and formed by constructive confrontations with a series of concrete problems. The character of the particular problems and the material and intellectual resources available to people dictated how they dealt with those problems. Afterwards, it was possible to assess how far they were successful and at what cost. Successes and failures left their mark. Human practical intelligence played an important role in the development of our activities.

Accepting the fact that important activities are neither creations of whim nor easily altered by fiat, some will still think that the historical particularity of the basis offered for norms of distribution militates against the possibility of a satisfactory account of them. There is a tendency to suppose that we have a satisfactory defense for values and norms only if these are shown to be valid for all people at all times in all circumstances. Why, though, can there not be rational defense of norms in terms of local conditions? This supposition clearly does not hold for all norms—why should we assume that it holds for norms of social distribution?

The idea that the norms of social justice must hold independently of existing activities and the local conditions that occasion them is reinforced by the worry that existing activities and the norms internal to them are themselves not sufficiently subject to criticism unless there exist independent norms. The argument might proceed in this way: Existing activities and their norms might be anything; they might sanction the most dreadful oppression of some individuals.

Unless there exist norms that lie outside of those practices, there is no way for the oppressed to sustain their claims that they are unfairly treated. Fortunately, there are such norms, including principles of fairness and justice, and people can appeal to them in criticizing existing practice.

T. M. Scanlon puts the criticism in this way: "Unless they are lucky, dissenters may not be able to say to the dominant group: 'Look! Your own principles make it wrong to treat us in this way.' What they then have to say is 'We are people too. How would you like to be treated in this way?' Those who wish to defend established social meanings will then need to respond in similar terms."[23]

The issue here is not whether one can enunciate plausible practical principles of very great generality and universality; obviously one can. There are practical principles—highly abstract ones—that apply widely over a variety of different activities and circumstances. It might be argued plausibly that some of these principles apply to all people in all circumstances. There is for example the principle that I have attributed to Aristotle: Social goods should be distributed in such a way that the reasonable claims of people for shares are recognized as far as it is possible to do so. Michael Walzer enunciates an eminently defensible principle that is intended to hold for all people at all times in all circumstances: "No social good X should be distributed to men and women who possess some other good Y merely because they possess Y and without regard to the meaning of X."[24] Another example is Frankena's principle of regularity and impartiality that requires that people not make ad hoc departures from established rules, that they treat similar cases similarly. Such principles as these are thought of as applying everywhere quite generally, whatever the local activities and purposes may be.

There is no question that there are such abstract norms as these, but it is by no means clear that they are independent of actually existing activities in the desired sense. Their generality can be explained by the fact that departure from these norms introduces conflict and confusion in the collective pursuit of any kind of activity. These principles, moreover, refer, implicitly or explicitly, to ex-

23. T. M. Scanlon, "Local Justice," *London Review of Books*, September 5, 1985, pp. 17–18.
24. Michael Walzer, *Spheres of Justice*, p. 20.

isting activities in such a way that a knowledge of the latter is necessary in order to able to interpret these principles and apply them. Aristotle's principle requires for its application an understanding of how reasonable claims are identified and weighed against one another, and this is a matter that requires knowledge of specific activities. Walzer's principle requires for its application an understanding of the socially established "meanings" of various goods, which in turn depend upon what people do with these goods, what roles these goods play in their lives. There exist abstract practical principles, but when these are separated from particular activities, they are vague and unhelpful—like the principle that all people in all circumstances should do what, all things considered, is best. An understanding of any norm, including these abstract ones, involves knowing how to apply them to a range of activities, and this will involve knowing how to apply the norms—together with any other norms that pertain. Only when an abstract norm is infused with this sort of knowledge does it escape being unspecific, unhelpful, and uninteresting.

Scanlon suggests that some version of the Golden Rule provides the desired sort of activity-independent standard for the assessment of existing institutions, practices, and norms. It is by no means clear, however, that various versions of the Golden Rule can be understood and applied without a broad grounding in a variety of existing activities. No one believes that we are everywhere forbidden to act toward people in ways that they do not like. 'How would you like to be treated like that?' and 'We are people too' must be understood against the background of a certain set of norms about how people should be treated. The convicted criminal might say this to the judge in protest against the sentence passed, but the Golden Rule may not apply here. Nor does it always apply when one's cherished property is forfeited for non-payment of debts or when one loses in a competition for a prize that one desires with all one's heart.

If particular activities and the norms internal to them were compartmentalized, if practice in one area had no effect on anything else, then the resources for criticizing activities and the norms internal to them might be limited. In fact, though, our activities are endlessly interconnected and entangled. As a result, there tends to be an abundance of norms for critical assessment of a particular activity. In the matrix of activities that makes up the life of our community, individuals and groups who are oppressed by existing practice may have much to fear, but they need not fear a lack of grounds for complaint. Their complaints will be futile unless they appeal to principles and standards that their fellows are committed to.

When we encounter a people who make it their practice to burn widows alive on the funeral pyres of their husbands, we want to be able to say: Whatever their other activities, norms, and purposes are, they should not treat people in this way. Nothing, however, prevents us from saying this. The important point is whether saying this is likely to get these people to stop burning widows. If it does not, it is unlikely to make any difference to add that universal moral norms indicate that this practice is abominable. We may suppose that we are articulating universal moral norms that apply to everyone, whatever their way of life, but it is apt to appear to our hearers that we are doing something more parochial. If we want to get them to stop burning widows, we must either use force on them or seek arguments that will make a difference to them. The latter course will require us to understand their activities, purposes, and norms, their way of life. Such an inquiry will require effort and patience, and nothing guarantees that it will culminate in the desired effective arguments. We may then have to rescue endangered widows by force and risk the disconcerting possibility that they will not be unreservedly grateful for our interference. Claims about what norms hold *sub specie aeternitatis* will not avail us. The problem is that what we require are norms of the proper kind that *these people* recognize as authoritative.

The words, 'But existing practice might be anything,' may seem to express an objection to a view that grounds norms in activities, but the force of the objection is elusive. It is true in some sense that we can imagine all of our activities being very different from what they are. There exist, moreover, other communities that actually have very different practices. It does not follow from any of this, however, that we cannot find rationales for our particular practices and standards for their critical assessment. If the objection is understood to mean simply that existing practice is arbitrary or that its norms lack authority, then the claim is false.

7. Vexed Cases and the Owl of Minerva

What does the view of ethics described in the preceding chapters indicate about how we should approach a bitterly contested contemporary issue such as abortion? The view itself does not claim to provide a recipe for an easy answer to the problems engendered by abortion or even explicit instructions for a difficult route to a solution. Moral philosophy cannot offer "a method," in the sense of an algorithm, for solving difficult problems. Rather, we are directed to examine the particular considerations at stake in each problem, consider what these factors mean in terms of the roles they play in our lives, and seek ways of solving the problem that somehow respond to all the relevant considerations. This instruction, by itself, does not appear to carry us very far toward a resolution of the abortion controversy. It is offered, however, against the background of the account that supports it; the resolution of the problems does not exist "out there" to be discovered. Rather, we must make it, and the materials out of which a solution is to be crafted are the considerations implicated in the particular problem itself, the problem's historical context, including our existing practices with their norms and purposes, and more or less similar problems that we have already resolved. A better solution will enable us to get on with whatever the problem interrupted, while preserving (and possibly reinforcing) as far as possible the various norms, values, and interests at stake in the issue.

If the foregoing account is correct, then it offers at least this much help with the concrete problem: We do not waste our time looking for the ready-made solutions promised by certain sorts of ethical theories, and we have a description of what the desired solution would look like. This latter point is important in the case of abortion, because, in fact, we actually have a proposed solution to the problem that fits reasonably well the description of a solution that is better rather than worse. That we presently have such a solution is not sufficiently appreciated, and this is at least partly because many people have inadequate notions about what an acceptable solution to the problem would look like.

That people should be divided about some bitterly contested issue, while there exists at the same time—right before their eyes—a good resolution to that problem and a rationale for it, is not an unprecedented situation. England in the seventeenth century was deeply divided about matters of religion and about the issue of what the attitude of the state should be toward religious questions. In fact the materials for a strong case for the civic toleration of religious diversity existed at the time, and some individuals glimpsed this possibility. It was hard, though, to separate the more important from the less important issues; confusion, emotion, and diverse parochial interests obscured the matter.

Even John Locke, who understood the case for religious toleration as well as any of his contemporaries, produced vexed, labored writings on the topic. Locke's justly famous *Letter Concerning Toleration* was written in 1685, well after England had adopted a certain degree of state toleration in religious matters. Still, Locke struggles in this work. It is clear that Locke understood that the domains of religion and politics were different, and that actual attempts to subordinate one to the other had results severely detrimental to one or both activities. Locke articulated the perception that religion had ceased to be a public matter and had become instead a matter of an individual's spiritual health and welfare, a private matter.[1] The exis-

1. John Locke, *A Letter Concerning Toleration*, ed. James H. Tully (Indianapolis, Ind.: Hackett, 1983), pp. 27 and 33. For a brief account of how religion ceased to be viewed as a public matter, as a community's resource for averting calamities such as famines and plagues, and became instead a private matter, an individual's means for achieving happiness and salvation, see John Dewey, *The Public and Its Problems* (1927). This can be found in *John Dewey: The Later Works, 1925–1953*, vol. 2, ed. Jo Ann Boydston (Carbondale: Southern Illinois University Press, 1984), pp. 266–67.

tence of the actual entanglements of church and state in his time and the persistence of the exceedingly ancient idea that any departure from religious orthodoxy somehow imperiled the whole community made it very difficult to grasp the case Locke struggled to make.

1

The solution I have in mind to the problem of how we should as a community view abortion is implicit in the 1973 United States Supreme Court decision in *Roe v. Wade*.[2] The latter is a legal decision; its assessment as a legal decision belongs to the field of constitutional law, and I will not be concerned with its adequacy as a proper interpretation of the U.S. Constitution. The Court, however, viewed the question of the constitutionality of various state laws prohibiting abortion as arising from a conflict of two important considerations. The solution proposed by the majority in this decision offered a resolution of this conflict.

In considering the constitutionality of a Texas statute prohibiting abortion except to save the mother's life, the Court recognized that the state had a legitimate interest in protecting prenatal human life. At the same time, the Court found, there is a constitutionally protected "right of privacy" that includes a woman's right to terminate a pregnancy. This right, however, is not absolute; a state might abridge this right in order to protect a sufficiently weighty state interest. The question whether a statute prohibiting abortion is constitutional turns upon the question whether there is a sufficiently compelling state interest in protecting prenatal human life—one compelling enough to justify the restriction of the right of privacy entailed by the legal prohibition of abortion. The Court could find no reason to view a prenatal human being as a "person" in the sense that this word has in the Constitution, and therefore rejected various arguments that abortion is appropriately prohibited as homicide. The Court argued that as a prenatal life develops, the state's proper interest in protecting it develops; the interest at the same time grows more weighty and substantial. Early in a pregnancy, this interest of the state

2. *Roe v. Wade*, 410 U.S. 113 (1973).

is not sufficient to outweigh the woman's constitutionally protected right of privacy. As the fetus develops, however, the state's interest develops too; at a certain point the importance of this interest surpasses the woman's right of privacy. The prohibition of abortion prior to this point would violate this right of privacy; after this point, however, the state would be justified in prohibiting abortion in order to protect the prenatal life. The Court maintained that this point where the state's interest in protecting prenatal life transcends the importance of the woman's right of privacy occurs when the fetus becomes "viable," capable of living outside the womb. Since the Texas statute prohibited abortion before viability, the Court concluded, it violated the woman's right of privacy, and thus was unconstitutional.

2

The legal decision in *Roe v. Wade* suggests a position on how we should think about abortion as a moral issue. The issue is one of conflict between considerations of the greatest moment. On the one hand, there is the increase of control over an individual's own life that is afforded to one half of the human race by the ability to choose to terminate a pregnancy once it has begun. The development of safe medical methods of terminating pregnancy means for women a substantial increase in freedom. This in itself is important. At a time when many women seek equality with men in many areas of life, abortion represents, in addition, the ability to counteract the unequal burden that their reproductive function places on women.

The artificial termination of a pregnancy, however, generally results in the extinguishing of a prenatal life. A prenatal human being, which would in the natural course of things develop into the woman's child, is destroyed. Our interest in protecting prenatal life is manifest. Our ability to make other human persons is miraculous, the difficult task of nurturing and educating a child is among the most important and satisfying we can undertake, and the existence of children in our community to whom we can transmit our culture adds immeasurably to the meaning and purpose of our own lives.

The community project of fostering ever-wider opportunities for all members to develop their capacities, begun hundreds of years ago, is not one we can or should give up. At the same time, our respect for and cherishing of procreation and the value of human life should be cultivated and promoted. In the contemporary problem of abortion, these considerations, these norms, are in direct conflict. The increment in autonomy that abortion provides can be realized only by destroying some prenatal human beings, and these beings can be protected only by denying women an important measure of control over their reproductive lives.

To declare one of these conflicting considerations sacred while ignoring the other is a plain mistake. To accept the result that in the abortion problem, one of these considerations must, however regretfully, be sacrificed to the other is to admit defeat of a sort. A course of action with respect to abortion that managed somehow to respond in a significant way to both norms, on the other hand, would be a preferable solution. The majority decision in *Roe v. Wade* provides a model in the realm of constitutional law for such a solution to the abortion problem in the related area of ethics. To apply the model, we think of the moral and practical importance of our interest in protecting prenatal life as something that develops as the fetus develops. In the early stages of a pregnancy, a woman might be justified in terminating the pregnancy for a range of serious reasons having to do with the whole conduct of her life. Having the child might in the circumstances entail long-term difficulties for her that she finds unacceptable. As the fetus develops, however, it requires more and more weighty reasons to justify destroying it. At some point during a pregnancy, this interest in protecting the fetus attains a degree of importance, of practical weight, that, in effect, surpasses the woman's autonomy as it is implicated in the ability to terminate the pregnancy. Before that point, for sufficiently serious reason, a woman would be justified in terminating her pregnancy, despite the value of what is thereby destroyed. After that point, however, the importance of protecting the developing life transcends that of the woman's autonomy, and abortion would be justified only in exceptional circumstances— in cases where it was required to save the woman's life or health.

Since the circumstances in which a pregnant woman might consider terminating the pregnancy are endlessly varied, and the weight of reasons for an abortion in many cases is hard to assess, it is difficult to describe policies in this area. There is a real need for a kind of casuistry here that provides some paradigms for use in hard cases. Many cases will arise requiring separate consideration. This is one of the factors that indicates that if aborton early in pregnancy is to be legally permitted, the decision of when an early abortion is appropriate should be left to the individual(s) most concerned. This is the rationale for abortion on demand.

The legal policy that is indicated by this position is permitting abortion on demand early in pregnancy and prohibiting it, except in specified extraordinary circumstances, after a certain point in the development of the fetus. Such a policy gives women a significant degree of control over their reproductive lives and at the same time gives substantial recognition to the moral and practical importance of prenatal human life. Each of the conflicting norms receives much more than perfunctory or merely symbolic recognition in such a solution. Both considerations have very real practical effect that results in a realization of the values implicated in them. The policy reaffirms these norms while adjusting them so that both can be observed simultaneously in the solution of this vexing problem. The solution harmonizes these conflicting norms in a course of action that expresses the meaning of both. It illustrates John Dewey's description of a reasonable choice as "one which stimulates by unifying, harmonizing, different competing tendencies. It may release an activity in which all are fulfilled, not indeed, in their original form, but in a 'sublimated' fashion, that is in a way which modifies the original direction of each by reducing it to a component along with others in an action of transformed quality."[3]

3

It is objected, of course, that for very good reason we do not allow people, in order to enhance their own autonomy, to kill other people. Abortion involves homicide, the objection continues. To countenance such killing, even when it is restricted to the earlier stages of pregnancy, is so to violate the meaning of the prohibition against homicide that the proposed solution is manifestly unacceptable.

3. *Human Nature and Conduct* in *John Dewey: The Middle Works, 1889–1924*, p. 135.

When confronting versions of this objection, the majority in *Roe v. Wade* found that a convincing case was not made for the claim that destroying a prenatal human life was homicide. The Fourteenth Amendment to the Constitution forbids states to deprive persons of life without due process of law, but the Court could not find any compelling reason to suppose that the word 'person' here (or anywhere else in the Constitution) was meant to apply to prenatal human beings. Generally, the Court claimed, there are not conclusive reasons for supposing that human fetuses have the moral and legal status of postnatal human beings. They declined to abridge women's constitutionally protected right of privacy on the basis of the problematic claim that abortion involves homicide.

It would be desirable to go beyond the Court's agnosticism on the question whether prenatal human beings are persons for moral and legal purposes. A useful starting point is Mary Ann Warren's position that personhood is a moral rather than a biological concept.[4] When we consider in this context whether a fetus is a person, we are asking, in effect, whether such entities are members of human communities, entitled to the protections and immunities that members extend to one another. Central to the issue of membership is the capacity to lead a life informed by norms and values. It is the absence of this capacity that explains why brute animals, despite their place in human life and their frequent claims upon our affections, still are not members of human communities, not persons.

Such reflections as these lead Warren to conclude, in effect, that a human being is not a person until that individual has the actual capacity to understand and be guided by norms. Since human fetuses lack such a capacity, Warren argues, they are not persons. Unfortunately, this position implies that postnatal human beings who have not attained the age of reason are not persons either. Killing an infant or perhaps even a very young child, then, is not killing a person, is not homicide either.

This last result is highly implausible. Infants and young children are not only full-fledged members of the community, but, because of their immature and vulnerable state, they are entitled to special con-

4. Mary Ann Warren, "On the Moral and Legal Status of Abortion," *Monist* 57 (1973), 43–61.

sideration and protection. Infants may be comparable to brute animals in that neither has the ability to understand and follow norms, but there is an obvious difference between a normal human infant and a dog or cat. The former will very quickly develop the capacity to participate fully, actively, in a life structured by learned activities and norms whereas the latter never will. If, however, the difference between infants and brute animals that qualifies the former but not the latter for membership in the community is infants' potentiality to develop the capacity to understand and follow norms, then prenatal human beings qualify as members too.[5]

The logic of this way of looking at the question of membership in the community forces one to choose between two implausible positions. Of course, there would be no community without members who actually exercise the capacity to be guided by norms. There is good reason, however, for extending membership to certain classes of individuals who do not have this capacity, and nothing requires that there be only one such reason.[6]

When an infant is born, it commonly is from the outset a member of a family. At first, it is not capable of being a participating member of the family, but the more mature members of the family treat the infant as though it had a central role, a significant place in family life. The infant is treated as a person, even though the infant cannot at first actively play this role for its own part. We do this, and we do this with feeling and conviction. We believe the infant is a special person, and our actions and feelings with respect to this individual reflect this belief.

Of course, accepted family practices with respect to newborn babies may be pointless—even inconsistent with other things we believe and do. Why should we quite systematically treat small infants as people and members of the family? Why should we not instead wait until they have developed capacities to understand and partic-

5. This is the position of Alan Donagan in *The Theory of Morality* (Chicago: University of Chicago Press, 1977), pp. 168–71.

6. Adult human beings who, through illness or injury, lose the capacity to guide their actions by norms do not cease thereby to be people. Rather, they are severely damaged, incapacitated people who are entitled to special consideration. The rationale for this position is connected with the norms of care for the ill and injured. The status of adults thus incapacitated is sufficiently different from that of prenatal human beings to warrant separate discussion.

ipate in norm-governed activities and *then* accept them and treat them as people and members? Consider: Small infants are unable to understand language and to talk. Yet members of their families and others talk to them continually. Would it not make more sense to wait until infants develop the ability to understand and speak the language before we talk to them? We teach an infant to talk by talking to it. There is good reason to suppose that in order to learn how actively to play the role of party in a conversation, of speaker of the language, an infant must be placed passively in that role by others. Gradually, the infant learns in this way to be an active participant. Similarly, infants learn actively to take part in a great many complex activities, to be guided by the pertinent norms, by being treated as participating members—even though they are not at first able to participate actively.[7] It is important that we treat infants as persons, as members of various communities, in order for them to learn to be participating members of these communities. There is no such rationale for treating dogs and cats as persons.

We regard infants as persons who are members of the community from birth, and there is reason to suppose that such an attitude and the actions that go with it are an important condition for infants' developing specific capacities to understand and follow norms, to play the roles of active members of communities, to live actively a human life. This practice is an important part of the early nurture and education of human beings. It is not feasible in the same way to place prenatal human beings passively in the role of members of the community. There is literally a wall between the prenatal human being and the social world with its life structured by norms. There is, then, not this reason in their case for regarding them as persons, as members. It is physically impossible to place them passively in the role of participants.

Much of our legal and other practice indicates that we become members of a human community for the first time at birth. There is at least the rationale just explained for that state of affairs. For legal and moral purposes, for social purposes generally, we come to be as

7. In developing a particular complex set of more or less harmonious active capacities to engage in norm-guided activities, a human child develops a character, a personality. The particular personality an individual develops will reflect his or her particular experience.

persons at birth. The proposal to extend membership in the moral community to prenatal human beings cannot be supported in the same way.

4

There is the argument, however, that prenatal human beings in the late stages of development are so like neonates that it is difficult to withhold from the former the attitude of cherishing respect that is appropriate toward infants.[8] On the other hand, a human conceptus is vastly different from a human neonate. It is difficult to imagine placing a tiny undifferentiated mass of cells in the role of passive participant in social life. The idea that as a prenatal human being develops, it becomes increasingly difficult to justify destroying it draws plausibility from these considerations. In the later stages in its development, it is so infant-like that we cannot withhold from it the feelings and attitudes evoked by neonates. We cannot accept the idea that it might properly be destroyed even to preserve some important life-option for the woman who carries it. How, though, are we to choose a point in fetal development at which our interest in protecting the prenatal life surpasses considerations of the woman's autonomy? The development of the prenatal human being is gradual—there are apparently no quantum leaps in the process of its becoming ever more like a human neonate.

The issue is in a way like the issue of when people cease to be minors and attain their majority. Individuals gradually acquire the ability to direct their own lives. For certain legal and other purposes, we need to indicate a precise point at which individuals reach their majority, but it is difficult to make a case for the eighteenth birthday rather than the twenty-first. It is important to keep in mind that a considerably stronger case can be made against choosing an individual's sixth birthday as the inception of majority and that a similarly cogent case can be made against setting the point of inception as late as the fortieth birthday.

8. Jane English, "Abortion and the Concept of a Person," *Canadian Journal of Philosophy* 5.2 (1975), 233–43.

For legal purposes in regulating abortion, we seek a point early enough in development so that the fetus is sufficiently unlike a neonate, but late enough so that a woman is able to retain a significant opportunity to decide whether to terminate the pregnancy. Perhaps twenty weeks is an appropriate point. Perhaps there are reasons why sixteen weeks or twenty-four weeks would be preferable to twenty. Much stronger reasons indicate that any of these points would be preferable to four weeks or twenty-eight weeks.[9]

This is an outline of the case that exists for the position that a pregnant woman might justifiably decide to terminate her pregnancy, provided that she has sufficiently serious reason to do so, and provided she effect her decision early in the pregnancy. What constitutes a sufficiently serious reason is a topic that requires a discussion of a variety of cases; it involves weighing a certain reason against such things as the value of a developing prenatal life; there are many hard cases.

5

A most serious barrier to accepting the foregoing as an outline of a solution of the vexed problem of abortion is that it countenances the sacrifice of a prenatal human life in order to permit someone to exercise her autonomy. Human life is too important, too precious to be used in this way, it will be argued. The response to this objection is, first, that the analogy of homicide ("killing babies") is not available to the objector here.[10] What is at issue is the importance of pro-

9. French law permits abortion in the first ten weeks if the pregnant woman declares she is "in distress." A 1976 West German law permits abortion within the first twelve weeks if the pregnancy is a serious hardship for the pregnant woman and up to the twenty-second week in cases of serious fetal deformity. See Ronald Dworkin, *Life's Dominion* (New York: Knopf, 1993), pp. 63–67.

10. Ronald Dworkin notes that most anti-abortion proponents do hold that abortion is justifiable when the pregnancy is due to rape or incest and when it is necessary to save the pregnant woman's life. He notes correctly that this position would not be sound if killing a fetus is killing a person. He takes this as evidence that such people do not really believe that a human fetus is a person. It is more likely, though, that people are simply confused about this matter. They do and they don't think of a fetus as a person. Their beliefs are inconsistent, and their tendency to think of a fetus as a human child or a homunculus reinforces their sense that abortion is generally morally wrong. See Dworkin's *Life's Dominion*, chap. 2.

tecting the prenatal life, a matter of genuine practical moment, in conflict with the increment of autonomy to women that the availability of a safe abortion procedure affords. One writer describes what is at stake in this increment of autonomy in the following words.

> Women need the freedom to make reproductive decisions not merely to vindicate a right to be left alone, but often to strengthen their ties to others: to plan responsibly and have a family for which they can provide, to pursue professional or work commitments made to the outside world, or to continue supporting their families or communities. At other times the decision to abort is necessitated . . . by the harsh reality of a financially irresponsible partner, a society indifferent to the care of children, and a workplace incapable of accommodating or supporting the needs of working parents. . . . Whatever the reason, the decision to abort is almost invariably made within a web of interlocking, competing, and often irreconcilable responsibilities and commitments.[11]

The advantage of the solution proposed over certain popular alternatives is that it permits us to give meaningful effect to both considerations. The objector is convinced, however, that the prenatal life is too precious to be sacrificed for an increment of autonomy, even a substantial one. The consequences of the policy the objector favors would be a world in which a significant increment of autonomy for women is denied. Of course, another consequence would be that prenatal life is protected at all cost. What shows that this policy would be worth this cost? The policy does emphasize the value of prenatal life. The solution I have defended, by contrast, effects an appreciable degree of protection of prenatal life *and* affords a measure of autonomy for women that represents an important step toward equality. This solution is, so far, better than the solution the objector proposes.

Is the protection of prenatal life afforded by the solution defended enough? The practical considerations we consult in con-

11. Robin West, "Taking Freedom Seriously," *Harvard Law Review* 104.43 (1990), 84–85. This passage is quoted in Dworkin, *Life's Dominion*, pp. 57–58.

ducting our lives do not come with numerical weights attached to them, indicating their relative importance. Their relative importance has to be determined. How much protection of prenatal life is enough? A prenatal human life is the result of our marvelous procreative ability, it is potentially someone's child, potentially a member of our community—it is potentially someone. It would be exceedingly crass to fail to appreciate these goods, but it would be crass too to fail to appreciate other goods. The solution defended affords a way of giving meaningful expression in practice to our appreciation of the value of prenatal life *and* of the value of the increment of freedom the availability of abortion provides women. Human fetuses are protected in the later stages of their development, when they are closer to their entry into the world and more like neonates. Abortion is permitted in such a way that a woman has sufficient time to ascertain that she is pregnant, reflect upon her options, and terminate the pregnancy if that is indicated. It is a better solution than one that preserves the value of one consideration at the cost of denying the other.

Deeply implicated in the complex of practices that constitutes our lives are a variety of different values and norms. Conflict among these values and norms is inevitable. In dealing with conflicting considerations, lawyers and philosophers talk of weighing and balancing these things, but these locutions can easily mislead. There is no scale on which the considerations in conflict in the abortion issue literally may be weighed. If, however, both are worthy of preservation, the obvious thing to do is to undertake to find a way to preserve both, a way that fits reasonably well with the related practices and the larger life of which the practices are components. Value pluralism is a fact, and it is a fact that these values are not always commensurable in any precise, systematic, straightforward way.[12] In seeking a solution to the abortion issue, it is important to keep these facts in mind.

12. In defending a position on abortion, I suggest some ways of comparing and "weighing" relevant conflicting considerations as they present themselves in this problem. I am not saying that these considerations are in no way commensurable. For a discussion of various senses in which different values might be said to be commensurable, see James Griffin, *Well-Being: Its Meaning, Measurement, and Moral Importance* (Oxford: Clarendon Press, 1986), chap. 5.

Is the defended solution the *right* solution to the abortion problem, though? There *may* be other possible solutions that somehow realize to an even greater extent than the solution defended both of the values at stake. Unless we have some inkling of what this even better solution might be, however, the defended solution is the one we should adopt; it is, as far as we know, the right one. The solution provides a way of responding to both of two conflicting considerations—a way that manages simultaneously to give significant effect to both. It moves us toward a state of things in which we can foster the ability of women to develop their capacities, while we at the same time express our appreciation of what prenatal life represents. The rightness of this solution is not a matter of its correspondence to a preexisting moral position already somehow in existence. Rather, it is a matter of making a solution to an unprecedented problem, one that preserves conflicting values by creating a new state of affairs in which all are as far as possible simultaneously realized.

This way of defending a solution to the abortion problem makes many people uneasy; they feel that somehow there must be more to solving the problem than finding a way of proceeding that somehow gives effect to both of the competing considerations. This sort of expectation, however, is one of the causes of the fruitless persistence of the controversy. There is no clear idea, even among very sophisticated people, of what a solution would look like.

The solution proposed leaves one with serious doubts. Will the practice of allowing the destruction of relatively undeveloped human fetuses lead to our depreciating the value of prenatal and neonatal human life? Will the practice lead us to exaggerate the importance of autonomy relative to other important values? We cannot answer these questions with certainty. There will, however, be comparable disturbing uncertainties with *any* proposed resolution of a matter of such moment as the abortion issue. In Frederick L. Will's words, we must give up "the now forlorn hope that somehow, somewhere, a magic philosophical formula will be devised that will enable serious philosophical minds to pierce, once and for all, the fog of indecision that attends ampliative governance when it is engaged with norms that broadly and deeply give form to our life and thought. The agitation, doubt, indecision, controversy, etc., are not ailments suffered, not symptoms of disease, but normally signs of health."[13]

It would be a mistake to suppose that the solution defended and this way of making a case for it somehow depreciate the importance and significance of the abortion problem and the things at stake in it. If we adopt this solution, we will have readjusted the collection of practical norms we have at the moment in such a way that we can continue meaningfully to observe them all in a situation where women increasingly want opportunities comparable to those enjoyed by men to develop their capacities. Safe and effective medical methods for terminating pregnancies are for the first time readily available. This creates a demand for abortion that conflicts with the sense that prenatal life is valuable, and the problem is to move in a way that preserves and even advances the important things at stake in the problem. To succeed in doing this would be a matter of the greatest moment.

What is at stake in any serious deliberation, John Dewey said, is "what kind of person one is to become, what sort of self is in the making, what kind of a world is making."[14] We, slowly, haltingly, continually remake our world. There is not a preexisting blueprint of what the world should be like to guide us, but we will nonetheless have to live in any world we make. The world involves the complex, intricately adjusted body of more or less well-functioning social practices that structure our lives and the ever-changing environment to which that body must adapt. The model of the living organism for the body of social practices is very apt here. It is for good reason that we have apprehensions and doubts as we pursue the project of remaking this world. There is wisdom, too, in Isaiah Berlin's advice that it is prudent to restrict ourselves in politics to the relatively modest task of resolving very concrete problems.

13. Frederick L. Will, "Philosophic Governance of Norms," *Jahrbuch für Recht und Ethik*, Band 1 (1993), 356.
14. John Dewey, *Human Nature and Conduct* in *John Dewey: The Middle Works, 1889–1924*, p. 150. See also Will, "Philosophic Governance of Norms," pp. 341–42.

Bibliography

Aristotle. *Nicomachean Ethics*, trans. Terence Irwin. Indianapolis, Ind.: Hackett, 1985.

——. *Politics*. In *The Politics of Aristotle*, trans. Ernest Barker. Oxford: Clarendon Press, 1948.

Arras, John D. "Getting Down to Cases: The Revival of Casuistry in Bioethics." *Journal of Medicine and Philosophy* 16 (1991), 29–51.

Baumrind, Diana. "Some Thoughts on Ethics of Research: After Reading Milgram's 'Behavioral Study of Obedience'." *American Psychologist* 19 (1964), 421–23.

Beecher, Henry K. "Scarce Resources and Medical Advancement." *Daedalus* (Spring 1969), 279–80.

Berlin, Isaiah. *The Crooked Timber of Humanity*, ed. Henry Hardy. New York: Vintage Books, 1990.

Bok, Sissela. *Lying: Moral Choice in Public and Private Life*. New York: Random House, 1979.

Callahan, Daniel. *Setting Limits: Medical Goals in an Aging Society*. New York: Simon and Schuster, 1987.

Carr, Albert Z. "Is Business Bluffing Ethical?" *Harvard Business Review* 46.1 (1968), 143–53.

Carroll, Lewis. "What the Tortoise Said to Achilles." *Mind*, n.s. 4, no. 14 (April 1895), 278–80.

Carter, Nicholas. "The Space Shuttle *Challenger*." In *Ethics and Politics*, ed. Amy Gutmann and Dennis Thompson, 2d ed. Chicago: Nelson-Hall, 1990.

Childress, James F. "Who Shall Live When Not All Can Live?" *Soundings* 53.4 (1970), 339–55.

Crigger, Bette-Jane. ed. *Cases in Bioethics: Selections from the Hastings Center Report*, 2d ed. New York: St. Martins Press, 1993.

Davis, Michael. "Thinking like an Engineer: The Place of a Code of Professional Ethics in the Practice of a Profession." *Philosophy and Public Affairs* 20.2 (1991), 150–67.

Dewey, John. *Art as Experience* (1934). In *John Dewey: The Later Works, 1925–1953*, vol. 10, ed. Jo Ann Boydston. Carbondale: Southern Illinois University Press, 1989.

——. *Human Nature and Conduct* (1922). In *John Dewey: The Middle Works, 1899–1924*, vol. 14, ed. Jo Ann Boydston. Carbondale: Southern Illinois University Press, 1983.

——. *The Public and Its Problems* (1927). In *John Dewey: The Later Works, 1925–1953*, vol. 2, ed. Jo Ann Boydston. Carbondale: Southern Illinois University Press, 1984.

——. *Reconstruction in Philosophy* (1920). In *John Dewey: The Middle Works, 1899–1924*, vol. 12, ed. Jo Ann Boydston. Carbondale: Southern Illinois University Press, 1988.

——. *Theory of Valuation* (1939). In *John Dewey: The Later Works, 1925–1953*, vol. 13, ed. Jo Ann Boydston. Carbondale: Southern Illinois University Press, 1991.

Donagan, Alan. *The Theory of Morality*. Chicago: University of Chicago Press, 1977.

Dworkin, Ronald. *Law's Empire*. Cambridge: Harvard University Press, 1986.

——. *Life's Dominion*. New York: Knopf, 1993.

——. "The Right to Death." *New York Review of Books*, January 31, 1991, 14–17.

——. *Taking Rights Seriously*. Cambridge: Harvard University Press, 1977.

English, Jane. "Abortion and the Concept of a Person." *Canadian Journal of Philosophy* 5.2 (1975), 233–43.

Euripedes. *Medea*. In *Euripides: Medea and Other Plays*, trans. Philip Vellacott. London: Penguin Books, 1963.

Finnis, John. *Natural Law and Natural Rights*. Oxford: Clarendon Press, 1980.

Flanagan, Owen. *Varieties of Moral Personality*. Cambridge: Harvard University Press, 1991.

Frankena, William K. "The Concept of Social Justice." In *Social Justice*, ed. Richard B. Brandt. Englewood Cliffs, N.J.: Prentice-Hall, 1962.

Freedman, Monroe H. *Lawyers' Ethics in an Adversary System*. Indianapolis: Bobbs-Merrill, 1975.

Fried, Charles. *An Anatomy of Values*. Cambridge: Harvard University Press, 1970.

Gillespie, Norman Chase . "The Business of Ethics." In *Profits and Professions: Essays in Business and Professional Ethics*, ed. Wade L. Robinson, Michael S. Pritchard, and Joseph S. Ellin, pp. 133–40. Clifton, N.J.: Humana Press, 1983.

Gorlin, Rena A., ed., *Codes of Professional Responsibility*, 2d ed. Washington, D.C.: Bureau of National Affairs, 1990.

Griffin, James. *Well-Being: Its Meaning, Measurement, and Moral Importance.* Oxford: Clarendon Press, 1986.

Hampshire, Stuart. *Two Theories of Morality.* Oxford: Oxford University Press, 1971.

Hart, H. L. A. *The Concept of Law.* Oxford: Clarendon Press, 1961.

Hume, David. *A Treatise of Human Nature* (1739). Ed. L. A. Selby-Bigge. 2d ed. revised by P. H. Nidditch. Oxford: Clarendon Press, 1978.

Irwin, Terence. *Plato's Moral Theory.* Oxford: Clarendon Press, 1977.

Jonsen, Albert R., and Stephen Toulmin. *The Abuse of Casuistry: A History of Moral Reasoning.* Berkeley and Los Angeles: University of California Press, 1988.

Kant, Immanuel. *Grounding for the Metaphysics of Morals* (1785), trans. James W. Ellington. Indianapolis, Ind.: Hackett, 1981.

Kipnis, Kenneth. *Legal Ethics.* Englewood Cliffs, N.J.: Prentice Hall, 1966.

Kuhn, Thomas S. *The Structure of Scientific Revolutions.* Chicago: University of Chicago Press, 1962.

Ladd, John. "The Quest for a Code of Professional Ethics: An Intellectual and Moral Confusion." In *AAAS Professional Ethics Project,* ed. R. Chalk, M. S. Frankel, and S. B. Chafer, pp. 154–59. Washington, D.C.: AAAS, 1980.

Locke, John. *A Letter Concerning Toleration* (1689), ed. James H. Tully. Indianapolis, Ind.: Hackett, 1983.

MacIntyre, Alasdair. *After Virtue,* 2d ed. Notre Dame, Ind.: University of Notre Dame Press, 1984.

Milgram, Stanley. "Behavioral Study of Obedience." *Journal of Abnormal and Social Psychology* 67.4 (1963), 371–78.

Mill, John Stuart. *Utilitarianism* (1863). Indianapolis, Ind.: Bobbs-Merrill, 1957.

Miller, Arthur G. *The Obedience Experiments.* New York: Praeger, 1986.

Murphy, Arthur E. *The Theory of Practical Reason.* LaSalle, Ill.: Open Court, 1964.

Nuland, Sherwin B. *How We Die: Reflections on Life's Final Chapter.* New York: Alfred A. Knopf, 1994.

Overton, William R. "Creationism in Schools: The Decision in *McLean versus the Arkansas Board of Education.*" *Science,* February 19, 1982, 934–43.

Patterson, Orlando. *Slavery and Social Death: A Comparative Study.* Cambridge: Harvard University Press, 1982.

Pence, Gregory E. *Classic Cases in Medical Ethics.* New York: McGraw-Hill, 1990.

Pincoffs, Edmund L. *Quandaries and Virtues: Against Reductivism in Ethics.* Lawrence: University Press of Kansas, 1986.

Plato. *Protagoras.* In *Plato's Protagoras,* ed. Gregory Vlastos. New York: Liberal Arts Press, 1956.

——. *Republic,* trans. G. M. A. Grube, revised by C. D. C. Reeve. Indianapolis, Ind.: Hackett, 1992.

Postema, Gerald J. " 'Protestant' Interpretation and Social Practices." *Law and Philosophy* 6 (1987), 283–319.

Rachels, James. "Active and Passive Euthanasia." *New England Journal of Medicine* 292.2 (1975), 78–80.

Rawls, John. *A Theory of Justice*. Cambridge: Harvard University Press, 1971.

Rescher, Nicholas. "The Allocation of Exotic Medical Lifesaving Therapy." *Ethics* 79.3 (1969), 173–86.

———. *Distributive Justice*. Indianapolis, Ind.: Bobbs-Merrill, 1966.

Ross, W. D. *The Right and the Good*. Oxford: Clarendon Press, 1930.

Rotunda, Ronald D. "Book Review: *Lawyers' Ethics in an Adversary System* by Monroe H. Freedman." *Harvard Law Review* 89.3 (1976), 622–33.

Sanders, David, and Jesse Dukeminier, Jr. "Medical Advance and Legal Lag: Hemodialysis and Kidney Transplantation." *UCLA Law Review* 15.2 (1968), 357–413.

Sartre, Jean-Paul. *Existentialism and Humanism*, trans. P. Mairet. Brooklyn, N.Y.: Haskell House, 1977.

Scanlon, T. M. "Local Justice." *London Review of Books* September 5, 1985, 17–18.

Sidgwick, Henry. *The Methods of Ethics*, 7th ed. London: Macmillan, 1907.

Steinbock, Bonnie. "The Intentional Termination of Life." *Ethics in Science and Medicine* 6.1 (1979), 59–64.

United States Supreme Court. *Cruzan v. Director, Missouri Dept. of Health*, U.S. 580 SLW 4916 (June 25, 1990).

———. *Roe v. Wade*, 410 U.S. 113, 93 S. Ct. 705 (January 22, 1973).

Veatch, Robert M. *Case Studies in Medical Ethics*. Cambridge: Harvard University Press, 1977.

Wallace, James D. *Moral Relevance and Moral Conflict*. Ithaca: Cornell University Press, 1988.

———. *Virtues and Vices*. Ithaca: Cornell University Press, 1978.

Walzer, Michael. *Interpretation and Social Criticism*. Cambridge: Harvard University Press, 1987.

———. *Just and Unjust Wars*. New York: Basic Books, 1977.

———. *Spheres of Justice*. New York: Basic Books, 1983.

Warren, Mary Ann. "On the Moral and Legal Status of Abortion." *Monist* 57 (1973), 43–61.

West, Robin. "Taking Freedom Seriously." *Harvard Law Review* 104.43 (1990), 43–106.

Will, Frederick L. *Beyond Deduction: Ampliative Aspects of Philosophical Reflection*. New York: Routledge, 1988.

———. "Philosophic Governance of Norms." *Jahrbuch für Recht und Ethik*, Band 1 (1993), 329–61.

Index

Index